A Perfect Discovery
Margaret Amatt

Scottish Island Escapes
A Quick Note

Welcome to the Isle of Mull – setting for the *Scottish Island Escapes* series

This series is loosely connected to The *Glenbriar Series* which is set after this series, but all the books can be enjoyed as stand-alones or in order – whichever you prefer!

There are some crossover characters throughout both series and hopefully you'll enjoy catching up with some familiar faces as well as meeting some new friends.

Happy reading!

First published in 2022 by Leannan Press

Second edition published 2023

Second edition published 2024

© Margaret Amatt 2022

The right of Margaret Amatt to be identified as the author of this work has been asserted in accordance with the Copyright, Designs and Patents Act 1988.

All rights reserved. No part of this publication may be reproduced, stored in a retrieval system or transmitted in any form or by any means, without the prior permission in writing of the publisher, nor to be otherwise circulated in any form of binding or cover other than that in which it is published without a similar condition, including this condition, being imposed on the subsequent purchaser.

All the characters in this book are fictitious, and any resemblance to actual persons, living or dead, is purely coincidental.

The Isle of Mull is a real island off the west coast of Scotland and most of the villages and sites mentioned in this story are real. Homes, farms, and other specific places and organisations are fictitious, and any resemblance to actual places or organisations is purely coincidental.

For more information on places in the story, please see the map at the back of the book.

Cover design Margaret Amatt 2024

eBook ISBN: 978-1-914575-83-9

Paperback ISBN: 978-1-914575-38-9

For he who wants to be an archaeologist when he grows up

Chapter One

Rhona

Rhona's fingers scrabbled in the dirt. The baking sun beat on her back. She grabbed her pick and chipped away at a layer of crumbling rock. *Take care.* In archaeology you only got one chance. She mustn't waste it.

A few more taps. She pushed away a strand of hair clinging to her sweaty forehead and tightened her ponytail before clearing the dust around the object and prising it out of its resting place. It may only be another piece of pottery but she was the first person to see it in over two thousand years.

Selecting her smallest brush, she gently swept it over the object. 'Wow,' she muttered, her heart racing. What an odd shape. Shell-like. Unusual. Could this be something big? For her career. Her hot, clammy fingertips clung to the find and she turned it carefully, examining it all over. This was like nothing she'd seen before.

'What have you found?' Annike peered up from her crouched position across the trench.

Rhona's hand trembled as she held out the object to her teammate. 'It's pottery but I think it's a shell.'

'Let me see.' Annike stood, tall and lithe. Crete in March was beautiful if you had time to lie on a beach all day, but out on the digs it was gruelling. Annike somehow managed to look cool as a cucumber. She examined the object closely. A frown grew on her pointy face.

'What do you think?' Rhona held her breath. *Please, let it be something good.*

'I'll take it to Simon,' Annike said. 'He should see this.'

'But... Hey, hang on—'

Annike strode off, her legs about ten foot long between the edge of her super-short shorts and her thick boots. Rhona hurried after her.

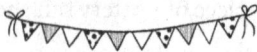

That evening, a fire crackled on the sand, tossing sparks at Rhona as she huddled her knees to her chest. Some of the team were still fooling about in the twilight, celebrating. Their laughter mingled with the wash of the ocean.

Her teammate Jay lay propped on one elbow, sipping beer. 'That was an awesome find. Just awesome. You know what we should do?'

'What?' Rhona asked.

'Let's all get a tattoo of a shell.'

Rhona laughed. 'Are you serious?'

'Why not?'

'Why not what?' Annike appeared at the fire wearing nothing but her bikini bottom.

'Jesus Christ,' Jay said. 'Do you have no shame?' He averted his gaze as she pulled on her t-shirt.

'No. But I don't have any boobs either. I'm flat as a pancake. You should go topless, Rhona. You've got the goods to show off.'

'Eh, I don't think so.' Rhona poked at the fire with a stick, tugging her knees closer.

'That shell is my ticket out,' Annike said. 'I'm sick of these long days, breaking my back.'

Oh, the glamour of archaeology. Rhona hadn't gone in with her eyes shut but, after five years working on digs, what had she accomplished? Except finding that shell. 'I found it, remember.'

'I haven't forgotten, but we're a team,' Annike said. 'I'm applying for site management jobs when the contract ends.'

'But isn't this only your second dig?'

'Yes, but I'm not wasting my life away.'

Rhona blinked. *Is that what I'm doing? Wasting my life away?* Annike was twenty-four and she expected a site management role. Rhona was twenty-eight and still 'just digging'.

'What were you saying when I came over?' Annike said.

Jay side-eyed her. 'Why don't we all get shell tattoos to commemorate our find?'

'Great idea.' Annike said, 'Let's do it. I saw a parlour in town.'

'You in?' Jay said.

'Em, well, I don't know.' Rhona ran sand between her fingers.

'You're the finder after all. The almighty finder of the shell of Crete,' Jay boomed like he was announcing it in the Parthenon.

'Go on,' Annike said. 'Guys like tattoos. Get one on your boobs and you'll have men crawling over you.'

'You're gross,' Jay said.

The wind carried off Rhona's sigh. She picked up her beer bottle and drained it. Every dig she'd done had thrown up a new set of friends but this group was her least favourite so far. They were in the same profession, they should have something in common, right?

'You love me really,' Annike said.

'No, I don't.'

'What about Rhona?'

Jay yawned. 'I'm not here to date.'

'Me neither,' Rhona said.

'No?' Annike said. 'But you're not seeing anyone, are you?'

'Nope.' *Thanks for the reminder.* Her love life was dire. Jay didn't do much on her internal "sparkometer" – something she'd invented as a teenager to rate her crushes. He was ok in a scruffy kind of way but like most guys she'd met, he barely rated above "acceptable" and didn't come close to Henry Cavill, her celebrity crush. Her previous relationships weren't exactly up there with *Romeo and Juliet*; drama and tragedy aside, they hadn't even led to anything steady. Who wanted a dirty digger of no fixed abode as a long-term girlfriend?

Annike persuaded Rhona to get the tattoo on the back of her shoulder, though Rhona kind of fancied it on her ankle. She went with it, but one glimpse of the needle and she fainted. Two hours and one revival later and the three of them plus team leader Simon emerged from the parlour sporting identical shell tattoos. 'All thanks to you, Rhona.' Simon beamed from ear to ear beneath his fluffy grey beard. 'My first tattoo at fifty-nine. My wife will kill me.'

'Oh no.' Rhona smiled at his mock horror. 'This is meant to be a celebration, not a sacrifice.'

'Ha, the sacrifice of Simon.'

Rhona linked her arm with him as they strolled along the traditional cobbled street. 'I'm sure your wife will love it.'

Simon patted her hand. 'Let's hope you're right.'

Annike volunteered to proofread the report on the shell and send it off. Rhona was grateful after spending days square-eyed at her laptop, making sure she got in every detail she could. She hadn't even started packing and only four days remained. If her contract was renewed, she would be back the following year, but she was investigating management positions on the off chance she'd get something last minute. The problem was always the same, however, nothing appealed to her inner romantic. She wanted to specialise in 3D reconstruction but competition was intense and jobs few.

On the penultimate day, they were summoned to a meeting with the dig director. Simon rubbed his palms together as he led his team towards the site office.

'Pity we don't get medals for this job. We're the star team.' He patted Rhona on the shoulder. The skin around the tattoo smarted and she winced slightly. 'Thanks to you.'

She hugged him around the waist.

'Oh, what's this for?'

'You're just a great team leader. I probably won't get to work with you again, but I'm glad I got to this time.' She adjusted her long blonde ponytail, her hair thick with dust. It needed a twenty-four-hour soak to regain its shine. Even that might not work.

'Oh, that's wonderful.' Simon grinned and fluffed his bushy hair.

Annike gaped with an expression of stunned disbelief. Obviously her liking for all things male didn't extend to almost sixty year olds whose dress sense was one step up from tramp.

The director shook hands with everyone before they sat on creaky fold-up chairs. A buzz of chatter thrummed in the dry heat. People making plans and moving on. Where would Rhona go next? She'd applied for a few jobs and hopefully her find would springboard her to greater things. She crossed her fingers and pushed them under her thigh. The director pulled out an iPad. 'Right, so Simon's team. Well done, you made the discovery of the year with the pottery shell.'

'Rhona pulled it out.' Simon puffed out his chest and pointed to her.

Her cheeks burned and she flapped his hand down.

'An amazing stroke of luck and a once-in-a-lifetime find.' The director checked his notes. 'We had a fantastic report on it too, which we'll be publishing shortly.'

Rhona couldn't stop smiling, her heartrate quickening with every word. Simon caught her eye and winked.

'I'd like to mention the following people who are moving on.' The director read out the names of researchers heading to pastures new. Rhona chewed her lip. Soon. A few more minutes and it would be her. 'And to Annike Steib, after her sterling work on this report, she's moving up to trench manager on our next dig.'

Annike's back was ramrod straight as she gave a nod, her smile more like a smug sneer. Rhona stared between her and the director. The thudding in her chest dulled, making way for a ringing in her ears. Wait... what? Had she misheard?

'But you wrote the report,' Simon whispered. 'Didn't you?'

'I did.'

'To the rest of you, it's farewell,' the director said. 'If you want to reapply for next season, we'll be happy to hear from you.'

Farewell? Reapply? Not even a renewed contract?

With a scraping of cheap metal seats on the container floor, Annike swanned out. Rhona got to her feet.

'Go after her,' Simon said.

A vice-like grip had taken hold of Rhona. Her shoulders tensed and she couldn't move her feet. 'But what can I do?' She didn't want to start a fight, not here.

'Come on.' Simon strode off.

Annike was outside, chattering and gesticulating wildly to some colleagues, that annoying expression still on her face. Rhona balled her fists, following Simon.

'Did you submit Rhona's report as your work?' Simon interrupted her mid-flow. Annike peered down her nose as though an irritating fly had landed on her arm.

'No. It was a collaboration,' she said.

Rhona's mouth fell open. 'I wrote the report. I found the shell.'

'That was luck. Anyone could have been in the right place at the right time. My interpretations were the important parts.'

'The ones I did. You were just meant to be proofreading it.'

'Did you send it in with your name on it?' Simon glared at Annike who towered over him.

'Like I said, it was a collaboration. We worked on it together. I was chosen for management because I have the skills.' She cast Rhona an utterly phoney apologetic look and moved away, restarting her conversation with the researchers.

'That sucks.' Jay folded his arms, frowning. 'Though I guess if you want to be successful you gotta shout as loud as her.'

Searing heat singed Rhona's cheeks and she swallowed. She could do with a drink of water... or something a lot stronger.

'I wonder if I can talk to the director about it,' Simon said. 'This seems highly unfair.'

Shaking her head, Rhona sighed. 'This is unbelievable. I trusted her and I was only ever nice to her.'

'That's because you're a nice person. Much nicer than her. A bit too nice in fact.'

Too nice? That didn't sound like a compliment. How had this happened? She'd made the find of her life but was standing here with nothing to show and nowhere to go.

Chapter Two

Calum

A clatter broke the quiet. Calum looked down at the cracked fragments of the blue pottery cup. Tea pooled across the oak laminate floor, and he clenched his free fist, taking a deep breath.

'Are you ok?' Rebekah's concerned voice asked from the phone.

'Just knocked over my mug.' He tsked. His mum had given him that as part of a set when he got his first property. *Ah well, never mind.* With a little shrug, he grabbed a dishcloth from the tiny kitchen corner of his revamped shipping container office. Typical, he had to break a nice one. 'Listen, I better go. I'll let you know more once I've investigated.'

'Ok, keep me posted,' Rebekah said.

Calum dropped the phone on the desk and stooped to mop the floor. Another mess. Much like everything else at the moment. He tossed the sopping cloth in the sink.

A knock on the glass door. He glanced around. The door clicked open and a smiling face peered in. 'Good morning.'

'Morning, Will. Watch the floor's wet. I just launched my tea over it.'

'Temper, temper.' Will placed his knuckles on his hips and shook his head. 'Why did you do that?' His boyish grin widened.

'It was an accident.'

'Oops.'

'Yup. But I've mopped it up.'

'You lead such a glamorous life.' Will smirked, closing the door behind him and perching on the spare desk in the corner.

'Don't I just. And it's not even ten o'clock.'

'The trials and tribulations of the Isle of Mull's favourite property mogul.'

'Hardly.' Calum swept up the mug shards and, with the smallest hesitation, dropped them into the bin. 'So, what are you doing here?' He thrust his hands into the pockets of his navy blazer and leaned back on his desk, crossing his long legs.

'I have a favour to ask,' Will said.

'Shocker.'

'What do you mean?' Will pressed his palm to his chest in mock offence. 'You think your oldest pal only visits you when he needs a favour?'

'Something like that. Now what is it?'

'It's the Midsummer fair next month and we're after donations for the raffle. So, what can property king Calum give us?'

'A contract to clean the Tobermory flats for a week?'

'Haha,' Will said, 'But no. How about a bottle of whisky?'

'Why don't you go down the hill and ask the distillery for that? If I give *you* a bottle of whisky, it'll never see the light of day again.' Will folded his arms and attempted a stern look.

'No? All right, fifty quid to spend somewhere on the island.' Calum ran his fingers through his short dark hair.

'Perfect.' Will pulled out his phone. 'I'll note that down.'

'Right, is that all?' Calum glanced towards the view behind the French doors. His luxury spend in the otherwise utilitarian setup. 'Because I need to get on. I have some information to email to Rebekah.' The tip of the iceberg on his crazy to-do list.

'Pity things didn't work out there,' Will said.

'They worked out fine.' Calum pulled out his seat and woke his laptop. 'We're friends and that's all we ever were.'

He ignored Will's sceptical expression. Rebekah was water under the bridge. Their dates had been ok. She was intelligent so the chat had been good. He'd liked her, yes, but the fire of passion wasn't there. Was it ever? His mum said he was too fussy. He disagreed, he just didn't enjoy intimacy, until he was sure he'd made a real emotional connection. There was the rub. How did you achieve that?

'Yeah, yeah,' Will said.

'Yes.' Calum tapped his middle finger on the desk. 'Now, seriously, Will. This is important. I got the planning department's email about the land at Kilnarkie.'

'Great. Have they granted permission for your house?'

'No.'

'Oh, that's a shame. Why not?'

'It has an archaeological condition attached.' Calum leaned his elbow on the desk and rubbed his chin as he scrolled the email again. Phrases leapt out at him. *Identified as a possible site of historical interest... Must be thoroughly examined... No building work should be undertaken...*

'What does that mean? Did they find bones or something?' Will shuffled in behind Calum and nosed over his shoulder.

'No. It's close to the old church and the planning department have decided there might be relics there or something. I don't really know myself. I only know it'll cost me a lot of money.'

'Don't the council pay for it?'

'As if. It's down to the developer to pay and have it thoroughly examined. It's a total minefield.'

'You're taking it well. I thought you'd be spitting feathers at a hold-up like this.'

Calum's chest burned; the feathers were ablaze inside him, but he held it in. 'I need to figure out what to do.'

'I wonder.' Will's face brightened like a light bulb had sprung into action on the top of his head. 'Why don't you ask Rhona Lamond for advice?'

Calum rubbed his fingertips into his sternum, his shoulders tensing around a growing pain. Did Will just suggest approaching one of the Lamonds? Why would a Lamond ever help him?

The land at Kilnarkie was only a couple of miles from their family home. They were more likely behind the hold-up. How like them to raise objections with the planning authorities about his land.

'Are you serious?' He glared at Will, stretching his shoulders, trying to ease the tension. 'Do you think I'd ever ask a Lamond to help me out?'

'Ah, come on, Calum. You don't still hold that grudge, do you?'

'Hold a grudge?' Calum inhaled as much air through his nose as he could and held it for a few seconds. 'Have you forgotten what they did to me... and you?' He tapped his pen on the desk, keeping his jaw set, forcing himself to breathe steadily. Will might be able to sweep the past under the carpet but he couldn't. The pain in his chest deepened and his heartrate notched up.

He swallowed, rubbing his ribcage, but there was no escaping it. *Arran Lamond was at the bottom of the concrete school stairs, lying there, motionless... Dead?* If that afternoon had never happened, how different things might have been. Calum might have finished school, met someone and been worthy of them, had a family of his own. His ribs ached with every breath. No. He'd never willingly work with a Lamond. Not now, not ever.

'I try not to think about those days.' Will's voice trailed off. He'd always been good at keeping his head in the sand.

Calum blinked away the visions of Arran Lamond prone and lifeless. His heart raced like he was still standing over him. *Is he alive?* Calum sometimes woke in cold sweats after nightmares. *What if he'd died?* His revenge on Arran, who'd been his best mate for a time, had been anything but sweet. The attack hadn't ended their troubles – as Calum had intended. It was just the start.

'Hell will freeze over and Scotland will win the World Cup before I let a Lamond loose on my land.' The words came out through gritted teeth.

'You're such a grouch. Why not forgive and forget? Rhona had nothing to do with any of it. She's a sweet little thing.'

'I don't even know who she is or why I would ask her in the first place.'

'You remember, she's Arran's little sister.'

'Not really.' And if he did, he was happy to forget. Erasing the Lamonds from his life was the ultimate step towards happiness.

'She's an archaeologist.'

'Good for her. I expect she's thousands of miles away digging up the tomb of Tutankhamun.'

Will chortled.

The Lamonds could do whatever they wanted. Calum had chosen to stay on the island, as had Will and a couple of other school friends, but most had spread their wings and flown long ago.

Trees in the woodland area outside the office swayed gently, blocking the view down the hill to the sea and the village of Tobermory. Calum watched them, mastering his breathing. *Must stay calm.* 'I'm not calling some random Lamond back from wherever they are to investigate something on land belonging to her family's arch-enemy when I don't know her, have no desire to know her, and don't want any Lamond on my land. Ever.'

'You're funny. But no need to call her back, she's already here. I bumped into her a few weeks ago.'

'Bully for her. One more Lamond on the island. Bloody fantastic.' He flicked back to the screen, scowling at the email. If deleting it would remove the problem, he'd hit that little dustbin and erase the complication. Shame, nothing was ever that simple.

'Calum. Stop it. Honestly, the Lamonds are ok these days. I know better than most how awful Arran was at school, but let bygones be bygones. Rhona's a delight. She told me some fascinating stuff about Iron Age objects that have been dug up recently on Mull. I'm sure she'd be happy to help.'

'Will.' Calum's tone was low, and maybe red had flashed in his eyes because Will recoiled. 'I don't care if she's dug up a hoard of treasure from the dinosaur era. I'm not asking her. If you seriously think one of the Lamonds will do this out of the goodness of their heart, then you're deluded. Even on the off chance she agreed, she'd probably charge a mint and make sure she found enough to prevent me building anything there. I know how their minds work.'

'I'm sure she wouldn't.'

Calum clenched his teeth to stop grating them. Did Will seriously believe this was simply about the incident from school? Had he been that blind for the last sixteen years? Will wasn't the one they were gunning for any more. Maybe that made it easier to forget. Calum's entire life had been shaped by those arseholes. Shoving his success up their noses was the only satisfaction and respite from the constant harassment he and his family had suffered at their hands. Every property he'd built or extended had faced objections – and he knew who was behind it. Projects had been delayed for months because of their interference. His name was mud all over the island because of them and their lies.

'If you're so bothered about it, why don't I meet her and show her around? She doesn't need to know who the land belongs to. I could be your agent.'

Years of mastering himself almost exploded in two choice words but Calum held it together. 'No, thanks. Let's leave her to unearth Rameses and his dynasty.'

'Ok, if you say so, but this seems like a great chance.'

'I need to send this email.' Calum kept his voice level and gave Will a wave.

'Ok, Calum. Thanks for the donation. See you.' The French doors closed behind Will and Calum tossed his head back, letting out a silent snarl. Will's intentions were great but sometimes he was so bloody naïve. Calum flicked through the planning report again. Where to start? As he scrolled through a long list of archaeology consultants in Scotland, one thing was certain, no Lamond would be part of his life ever again.

Chapter Three

Rhona

Rhona's top stuck to her and she wiped sweat from her brow as her feet slapped the concrete. She tugged out her earbuds to listen to the sea lapping to her right. The heat reminded her of Crete last winter. From one island to another, though this one was home. At least for a little while. How ironic to be back living here after she'd sworn, when she left school ten years ago, she'd only return to visit family and friends. But without a home this was the best option – short term. She jogged on past the tiny sleepy harbour at Croig, stopping briefly to adjust her top, which kept riding up. Even with the best fitting sports bra, she jiggled too much. Seemed that way anyway. Not that anyone out here would see; the road was empty.

With a racing heart, she reached the front door of her parents' house, slammed her foot on the doorstep and leaned over, placing her hands on her knees. Rambling bushes flowering in the May sunshine grew in front of the stone wall surrounding the lawn. Bees buzzed around as she caught her breath.

A cyclist whizzed by on the tiny single-track road winding its way past the house.

Rhona clicked open the door of the whitewashed villa. Built about twenty years ago, Rhona's family had been the first to live in it. She whipped off her running shoes and put them on the rack in the front porch beside the other perfectly lined-up pairs. Her mum, Judy, liked to keep a handle on the cleaning. Mud on the floor would induce a hissy fit.

Rhona padded over the shiny wood floor into the kitchen to grab a drink.

Her dad, Alister, peered over his book from the kitchen table. 'What have you been doing to yourself? You look exhausted.'

'That was a tough run.' Rhona pressed a glass to the lever on the American-style fridge. Cool water splashed in. 'I'm out of shape. I can't run when it's too hot so I never did much exercise in Crete.'

'Just don't get obsessed, like some young people do.'

'I don't think I'll ever be obsessed with running.'

'Instead of overexercising, start looking for a job.' He closed his book.

Rhona sagged into a chair and stretched out her legs. 'I have a job.'

Alister stared at her with the same look he'd used on students for over forty years, right up until he retired from teaching maths last summer.

'What?' Rhona smiled back.

'It's not exactly what you signed up for.'

Too right. Her arms drooped at her sides. Doing research at home was worse paid than field work and that was saying something. Just as well she didn't do it for the money. 'It's keeping me busy for now. Until I find something better.'

'You just don't seem your usual self. We miss cheeky-chops Rhona.' He beamed like she was a ruddy-cheeked toddler. 'Why don't you consider consultancy work?'

'I don't have enough experience to be taken seriously. I'll be overlooked. There are lots of consultants with more going for them.'

'Oh, come now, you'll never get anywhere with that attitude. If you need experience, why not volunteer somewhere? I've seen a couple of community digs here the past few years.'

Rhona slumped a little further. So much of her working life had been volunteering it made a mockery of her degree.

'This is the career you chose,' Alister said. 'It was a tough one to get into but you did it, so now make the most of it. Look at your sisters.'

Of course, the obligatory comparison. Catriona had studied law and was a partner in a solicitor's office. Mhairi had done economics and was a management accountant.

'And Arran. He struggled with ADHD all through school and look at him now.' Alister beamed with pride. Arran was an insurance broker and always had a lot of cash.

Unlike me.

Rhona was the baby. Her sisters always saw her like that anyway. And then they'd fight. First over who would look after the cute and funny baby sister. Then about who wouldn't when they got older and couldn't be bothered. Her arrival had brought so much internal feuding. Rhona hardly saw them now.

'Where's Mum?'

'In her shed.' Alister jabbed his thumb over his shoulder towards a wooden summer house in the garden.

'I'll go see her.' Rhona left via the French doors in the dining room adjacent to the kitchen. Not bothering with shoes, she snuck across the soft lawn. The summer house doors were thrown wide open. The garden was on the slope of a hill covered with gnarled old trees. One of them had long branches hugging their old tree house. Rhona had climbed up on her second day back and given it a spring clean. Sitting inside, watching the sea was so romantic – if she could banish the vision of the time she'd caught Arran snogging a girlfriend in it. Some things were best forgotten. 'Hey, Mum.'

'Hello, darling. Where are your shoes? You'll get filthy socks.' Judy squinted over her easel, a palette knife poised in her grip.

Rhona scanned down and pouted. 'Honestly this is nothing, Mum. You should see the state of my clothes after a dig.'

'Let's hope I never have to. Archaeology is one of those careers that sounds better on paper. I love the idea of living history but all that dirt...' She wrinkled her nose.

Rhona pinched a fold-out chair from behind the door, plonked it on the grass and lounged on it. 'You're not wrong.'

'Oh! That tattoo.' Judy scrunched up her whole face this time. 'It's all I see when you're dressed like that.'

Rhona peeked over her left shoulder. She'd got used to it now, though she still wasn't sure why she'd let them talk her into it. She adjusted the strap on her white vest top. 'Is it that bad?'

'You should have it removed. You're such a pretty girl and tattoos are so harsh.'

'It's a shell, not a skull.' She craned her neck to nosey in the space her mum called the studio. 'Can I see what you're doing?'

'No.' Judy angled the easel firmly away from Rhona. 'You know I don't like people looking before I'm finished. You have your shower and let me finish. Maybe you could message Arran for me. Find out the exact dates he's coming back.'

Rhona returned her gaze to the sea. 'Ok.' She pulled out her phone and sent him a quick message. 'Would you like me to bring you a coffee or something to eat?'

'No, thank you.' Judy focused on the easel.

Rhona replaced the chair, leaning further in, trying to sneak a glimpse of the painting.

A hand landed on her shoulder and she spun around. 'Dad, you made me jump.'

'You just missed a call on the house phone.'

'Who was it?'

'Will Laird.'

'Who?' Rhona frowned for a second, blinking until a picture of a smiley man formed in her mind. 'Oh, him, I remember.' Why would he call her? He was a friend of Arran's from ages ago but she barely knew him. 'What did he want?'

'He didn't say but asked if you could call him back. I told him you would when you were decent.'

Rhona burst out laughing. 'He can't see me down the phone. And how am I not decent? This is running gear, it's not like I'm topless or anything.'

'Oh, really, Rhona.' A line creased Alister's brow. 'Will is married, he doesn't need any nonsense.'

'You're funny.' She gave him a playful pat on the arm.

'In all seriousness, watch what you say to Will. He's a pleasant enough chap but he's very friendly with the Mathesons.' Alister flicked Judy a loaded look.

A cloud drifted across the sun in the cool breeze, casting a shadow over the lawn and the studio.

'I remember.' Rhona rubbed her arms at the drop in temperature. A weight pressed on her chest with a faintly nauseous sensation. She'd been thirteen when the war started. Curled under her blankets, she'd waited. When would the click on the front door come? When would they be back from the hospital? Rain hit the windows and branches tapped the panes. She hated being home alone. When they finally came, she'd peered out her bedroom door. Mum and Dad led a bruised, swollen and wrecked Arran into his room.

'Go back to bed.' Mum's eyes were puffy and red.

'What happened?'

'Calum Matheson attacked him.'

Calum Matheson? Arran's friend. The tall quiet boy she'd crushed on for over a year.

Tears had soaked her pillow.

Now any mention of the name Matheson was greeted with vitriol and tension clouded the air like a noxious gas. The shop at the ferry port had been out of bounds since Rhona returned to the island. Calum's mum worked there, so they boycotted it.

Rhona let her eyelids drop and she sighed. Even then she'd had a knack for picking the wrong kind of guy. Maybe teenage crushes didn't count. 'I don't know the Mathesons now anyway, so it's not like I could say anything one way or another.'

'Awful people,' Alister muttered. 'Calum was a bright boy at school but such a temper and what violence. Now he's a money grabbing so-and-so, buying properties left, right and centre.'

'I hate him,' spat Judy. 'I always said we should have pressed charges when we had the chance.'

'I thought it'd be enough punishment living with what he did. Apparently not. He's only got more arrogant,' Alister said.

'Hasn't he just. I see him sometimes when I go to Tobermory, swanning about on his phone, making himself look important. The whole family have got so up themselves. Anne used to be a nice woman but after Calum,' Judy screwed up her nose, 'hurt

Arran, she wouldn't accept her perfect son had done anything wrong. The sun rises and sets on him as far as she's concerned.'

'And as for Ron,' Alister said. 'Looks like a thug. It's easy to see where Calum got his violent streak.'

A thug? Harsh way to describe him, but such was the Matheson effect. A rotund semi-bald man with tattoos became a thug. Calum looked nothing like him. Did he? He was skinny and dark-haired. But in sixteen years, he could have beefed out and lost his hair too. Rhona wouldn't know him if she saw him.

'Didn't he get married a couple of years ago?' Rhona rubbed an insect bite on her arm. 'Or am I thinking of someone else?'

'Calum isn't married,' Judy said. 'Looks like the man about town if you ask me. Strutting around putting it about all over the island, I expect.'

'There's no one who'd have him,' Alister said. 'Everyone knows what he's like.'

'Most women can see right through that kind of smarmy man.' Judy picked up her palette knife and made some sharp movements on the canvas.

Rhona raised a considering eyebrow. Calum hadn't looked smarmy at school. His face had been covered in terrible acne; he'd hidden more than strutted. She'd mooched along to the football club with Arran hoping to catch a glimpse of him. But he was never there. Was he too shy to show up in case people laughed at him? She'd dreamed of being the one to tell him it didn't matter and she liked him for the boy inside. She cringed. Thank god, she hadn't. The boy inside had turned out to be much worse.

'I'll have a shower, then I'll call Will.'

As she smoothed conditioner over her hair and brushed it through, she recalled bumping into Will a few weeks before. He'd been fascinated by the island's archaeology. He must have a question about that.

Once she was dry, she slipped on a pair of belted navy culottes, flattening them over her hourglass shape. Her white, scoop-necked t-shirt pulled taut across her chest and she grimaced, grabbing a cardigan, so she could cover herself in case Will had developed the superpower of looking down phone lines.

'Hi, is that Will Laird? It's Rhona Lamond. I understand you want to talk to me.'

'Ah, hello. Yes, I do.'

She held the phone away while he gushed with pleasantries and chatted about the weather. He sounded super cheery but when would he get to the point? 'Now, I need your advice,' he said. 'In a purely professional capacity, of course.'

Finally!

'Sure. What can I help you with?'

'I wonder if you would be able to check out some land. I'm curious to see if you think it has any archaeological significance.'

'Oh, right. Whereabouts?'

'Not far from your parents. Near the old church at Kilnarkie.'

'I can tell you straightaway, I'm sure it does have significance. Churches like that were usually built where there was habitation, so it's likely a settlement was there at some point prior to that. Mull is largely undiscovered as far as archaeology goes.' Undiscovered and crying out to be investigated. *By me!* If only. She had no right to go digging willy-nilly and it wasn't like people were throwing money at projects like that.

'I live across the bay,' Will said. 'Just outside Dervaig. Would you mind popping along to the land with me sometime? I'd like an expert opinion.'

She checked her watch. 'I could go now if that suited.'

Twenty minutes later, Rhona jumped into Will's maroon people carrier and he drove along the road she'd jogged that morning. When they reached a gate, she jumped out and opened it and they trundled up a stony track past some scattered holiday cottages.

'The owner of the land has had an archaeological condition attached to their planning application and I'd like some advice on it,' Will said. 'I've never heard of that before.'

'You'll need a consultant. Has anyone done a field walk or a survey?'

'Nothing so far.'

At the hill crest, the path disappeared except for a faint track through the grass, then the land opened onto to a green plain, surrounded by low hills, leading to a sandy beach with stunning views of the glistening sea and the outer isles of Coll and Tiree. She'd been here so many times as a girl, running across the machair with her friends, the wind blowing her hair. Hours had been spent on the nearby beaches, swimming, bodyboarding and collecting shells. Her chest swelled and warmth spread over her shoulders, flooding her veins with a sense of calm and well-being. This had to be her favourite place on the island.

'It's so beautiful.'

'Stunning,' Will agreed.

They got out of the car and Rhona followed Will up a slight incline over rough ground to a tumbledown bothy. 'This view is just...' She shielded her eyes, gazing at the emerald sea. No words could do it justice. 'I could sit here all day listening to the waves.'

'It's a mighty fine spot, all right.' Will zipped up his jacket and the breeze buffeted it.

Rhona scanned over the rambling area. 'Is the idea to replace this bothy with a new house?'

'Yes.'

'And where does the land start and end?' The undulations in the ground made her skin tingle. Possibilities lurked in those ridges and she'd love to investigate.

'I don't have the exact location but it goes right to the old churchyard, as far as that line of bushes.' Will pointed to his left. 'And right to the shore.'

'That's a big plot.' The old churchyard was a favourite childhood walk and, if memory served, it was some way back. 'You only need to excavate the part where you're planning to build. The rest of it can be left untouched.'

'Ah, that's good. My friend is worried about the cost.'

The breeze lifted Rhona's hair and she smoothed it back. Her scalp prickled and she bit the inside of her lip, twisting a strand of hair around her finger. 'Who is this friend?'

'Oh, you know.' Will tossed up his palms, his tone airy.

'It isn't Calum Matheson, is it?'

Will nodded.

'Then I have to go.' Blood throbbed in her ears and she wheeled around. Heat drained from her cheeks. *Must get out of here now.* 'Don't you remember what happened with Calum and Arran at school?'

'Of course I do, but it was a long time ago.'

'My family haven't forgotten and my parents will skin me alive if they find out I'm here.'

'Will they? I'm sorry to hear that.' Will scratched at his wrist.

'I don't want anything to do with him.' Adding to a family feud was the last thing she needed. 'It's not like his reputation has ever improved.'

'He's not that bad. In fact, he's not bad at all.'

'Someone's coming.' Rhona cocked her head at a hillwalker striding towards them. 'We should go.'

'Uh-oh.' Will rubbed at his chin, his eyes bulging but not straying from the hillwalker. 'I might be in a spot of trouble.'

Rhona frowned at him, then followed his sightline. The walker wasn't dressed for the hills: no backpack, no walking boots. He hopped across a few rough rocks and Rhona's pulse rate rocketed. This guy was smartly turned out... and handsome, though his expression was grim. A prickle of awareness stung her. 'Is that... Calum?' Her throat went dry and the word spiralled into the wind.

'Er, yes.' Will pulled an apologetic face.

That was what he looked like now? *Oh my god*. A cold sweat broke on her brow. She swiped at it with her fingertips. When he'd been a spotty teenager with gangly legs and a wiry body, she'd fancied him. Her heart thudded against her ribcage. He was getting closer and *shit*... His brows were knitted and his fists balled. But that strong jaw, his perfectly spaced eyes, the blazer, those well-fitting jeans – oh no. The sparkometer whizzed into action. Her insides ignited with a sizzling spark, the fire she'd been waiting for forever. But why did it have to be him? Not him. The world's most unsuitable man! No, no, noooo! He was almost upon them. How the hell could she get away or explain herself?

Chapter Four

Calum

Calum inhaled slow, steady breaths. His feet propelled him forward faster than his brain. What was going on here? Nothing good. Will and his crazy ideas. *Keep a stopper on it.* Or he'd blow up in Will's face. He couldn't allow that. Especially in front of someone else. His gaze flickered over the unknown woman. She crossed a white cardigan over her upper body and held it tight. Long blonde hair tumbled around her shoulders and her cheeks glowed pink. Was that…? In her eyes, he caught a flash in the blue. An unforgettable face swam to the forefront of his mind. Arran. That worthless dickhead. He'd been blessed with good looks too, like this woman.

Control. Stay in control. Calum clenched his fists. 'What brings you here?' He angled his shoulder, cutting out the woman and keeping his focus firmly on Will.

'Now don't get mad.' Will held up his hands.

Calum raised his eyebrows. 'Do I ever?' Bile rose in his chest, burning into his throat. If Will mentioned that school incident now, the restraint Calum had worked on for so long would shatter. He clenched his fists and trained his sight on Will.

'I want you to keep an open mind. This is Rhona.' Will shuffled in her direction, putting out his arms to invite her into their conversation. She didn't move.

Calum pulled his lips into a brief – and utterly fake – smile. 'Pleased to meet you.' He whipped back to Will. 'Why are you here?'

'Well, after our chat the other day—'

'The one where I made the situation perfectly clear.'

'The very same.' Will stifled a little cough with the back of his hand.

A pain spread through Calum's jaw as he fought to not openly grind his teeth. Why did Will think it was ok to do exactly as he'd said not to? If he would just stop grinning. This wasn't exactly funny.

'Excuse me,' Rhona said.

Calum dug his nails into his palm so hard it was like being attacked by a razor blade.

'I don't want to cause any problems here. All I was doing was having a look. I haven't touched anything.' She clung to her white cardigan, holding it close. The edges fluttered in the breeze.

Calum cast his eyes over her. A jolt of electricity hit him deep and he nipped his upper lip with his teeth. His mind rewound to a place he didn't usually go. Now he remembered. She was the little sister who'd dissolved into giggle fits every time she saw him.

It didn't take a brain surgeon to work out why. His acned face had always been a subject of great hilarity.

Her cornflower blue irises sparkled and her long lashes fluttered like she was still a giggly girl about to skip off to school. Calum threw back his shoulders. Those days were gone. He was a grown man with no blemishes on his skin. He blinked, dropping his focus to his feet until he summoned internal calm. Slowly, he raised his gaze. It travelled over the curve of her hips, hourglass waist, and ample chest. *Oh Christ.* Look somewhere else. Quick. His nerve ends blazed. Her immaculate teeth trailed across her bottom lip. She gave him a slight smile. His heart lurched about a hundred miles an hour. *Bugger.* They were supposed to be talking about something. *What?*

'That's, um, fine.' What had she said? Was he meant to be answering a question? *Eyes away.* He shifted his focus to a point in the sea, miles out, where breakers crashed over a rock, causing lashings of foam to spritz up.

'I'll go then,' she said. 'See you, Will.'

'Do you want a lift back along the road?'

Calum side-eyed them.

'No, I'm happy to walk.' She gave him a wave.

Calum forgot the sea view and tracked her as she trudged over the rough ground. Her hips swayed and her culottes flapped in the breeze, long hair tumbling down her back in wind-tangled waves. He tugged at his collar. Why was he so warm? His neck was burning up.

Will coughed. Calum snapped his gaze back to him, his chest simmering again. He narrowed his eyes and folded his arms. 'What did you bring her here for? I said no. I don't want the Lamonds having anything to do with my business.'

'But she's really nice. And I thought it might help. You always have so much on your plate.'

'It's my job. I can handle it. I don't go about doing your job for you.'

Will clapped him on the arm. 'Ah, Calum. I'm not doing your job for you. I just think you're missing a trick.'

Calum sighed. 'I appreciate that and if she was anyone else, I'd jump on her... I mean, jump on the opportunity.'

Will tossed his head back, roaring with laughter.

'Shut the fuck up.' Calum drew his hand over his forehead. *Shit, shit, and more shit.*

'Aye, I bet you'd jump her too.'

'I said shut up.' Calum glowered at him. 'What am I going to do here? This land has caused me nothing but trouble.'

'I'm not sure why you bought it in the first place. It's gorgeous but it's so out in the sticks.'

'To annoy the Lamonds.'

'Seriously?'

'No. I like it here. It's the perfect spot.' Though having the Lamonds' house not far away put him off living in it himself. But the land had a special feel. He didn't do vibes or anything like that but something about this place called to him. 'It doesn't look like it'll work out. I'm considering donating it to Rebekah's affordable island housing project. Thing is, I'm not sure it's suitable for that either. It's so remote and if there's any possibility of this being an important archaeological site—'

'Which there is,' Will said. 'Rhona just confirmed it.'

'Well, there we go.' Calum held up his palms. 'It's unlikely I'll get planning permission for even one house. And if it's for affordable houses, I need at least two on here, maybe more. Each one will need more investigating, making it less and less viable.'

'Yeah, it's tough. I'd love it if you lived here. Not too far from me. You could babysit when Will Junior arrives.'

'I'm not exactly a million miles from you as it is.'

'Ha, true!'

'How's Morven?'

'She's fine, just desperate to have the baby now.'

'Not long now. Give me a shout if you need anything.'

'Just the babysitting.' Will grinned hopefully.

'Maybe, when he's a bit older.'

'Ah, you mean you'll be naughty Uncle Calum who leads him astray.'

'That's the one.' Calum clapped Will on the shoulder. Holding a grudge was hard with that face beaming back and falling out right before his best pal became a dad would be pointless and petty.

'So, you're not mad at me?' Will asked.

'Like I said before, am I ever?'

'No, you're cool as a cucumber. Though maybe Rhona got those juices pumping for a moment there.'

'You always had a good imagination. Now bugger off back to your wife and annoy her for a change.'

Looming large in the spare bedroom of Calum's waterfront apartment in Tobermory was a fifty-kilogram grappling dummy. Calum rubbed his hands together, warming his palms. The whole room was kitted out as a home gym. Five minutes after getting home, he was dressed in his shorts and vest. Now the ugly dummy was going to be pulverised. As a karate black belt, Calum had the moves and he was good. Too good for Arran Lamond.

These days he reserved his fury for the dummy. And the uncontrollable: Will on his land with that woman. Kick. Kick. High kick. Punch. That woman. Rhona. *Christ*, why did she have to be such a looker? Kick. It would be much easier to forget her if she hadn't been so appealing. Punch. Punch. Kick. Those long lashes would be fluttering in his mind for some time yet. With a massive inhale, he launched a powerful thrust of his foot into the dummy's face.

Chapter Five

Rhona

'Thanks, Dad.' Rhona leaned over and kissed him as he pulled on the handbrake outside the Spa Hotel. At the entrance, her friend Kirsten waited, sweeping her long wavy dark hair over her shoulder. Rhona beamed and waved. It had been too long.

'Just give me a call when you need picked up,' Alister said.

'Thank you.'

'It's like you've never been away. Dad's taxi is back in business.'

'The best taxi service.' Rhona gave him another kiss until he flapped her off.

'On you go. Kirsten's waiting.'

Rhona jumped out the car. 'Hellooo!' She ran up the steps and pulled Kirsten in for a hug. 'How are you doing?'

'Great.' Kirsten gave Rhona's back a pat.

'It's the weirdest thing being back. I don't see you much more than I did when I wasn't living here.'

'A little bit more.' Kirsten pushed open the glass doors into the modern foyer. A bright chandelier twinkled overhead. 'We once went three years without seeing each other.'

'That's true and far too long. How are the tours?'

'Busy as always. That's why I haven't had a chance to meet before now.'

'That's ok.' Rhona stepped up to the high dark-wood reception desk. 'I imagine you want to spend time with that hot fiancé of yours.'

Kirsten smiled and a tinge of pink bloomed in her cheeks. 'Yeah. When we're both doing tours, we don't see a lot of each other.'

'I'd love to do one of his sea-plane tours.'

'They're so popular, they're always booked way in advance.'

Kirsten nodded towards the reception desk and Rhona turned around. A cheery receptionist greeted them and showed them into the spa area.

'You can change in here.' She opened a door and guided them through.

'I've never done a spa day before.' Kirsten dropped her bag onto a bench.

'I've done a couple.' Rhona glanced around the wood-panelled room. Stunning prints of Mull waters covered the walls. One very like the beach at Kilnarkie. 'Mum says this place is amazing.' She slipped off her jacket. 'I guess it's a place of no shame.'

'Girls together and all that.' Kirsten sat and pulled off her shoes.

'I worked with a woman on Crete who used to strip off all the time.' Annike. Ugh. Rhona's nails bit into her palms. That horrible woman. How could she have done what she did? Shameless cow. Rhona hadn't complained to anyone about the stolen report. What to say without sounding whiny and phoney? She hated conflict. If only she hadn't trusted Annike... or had been a better judge of character. 'She was a man-eater and a bitch.'

'Oh my god, she must have been bad, you never talk about people like that.'

'Yeah. She was awful to me. And she had the figure of a supermodel too, double bitch.'

'Wow, you really hate her.'

'I do.'

'But there's nothing wrong with your figure. You were always the pretty one in our group.'

'Aw, thanks, do you think so?' She skimmed over her hourglass shape in the mirror. Maybe it wasn't that bad. But clothes never sat right. Her waist was trim but her hips and boobs were wide so that tops stretched and waistbands needed cinched or they hung loose. Her last boyfriend hadn't been a fan of curves. He hadn't said so but it was obvious. 'That's kind. Annike made me feel so inferior.' And she was a thief. *Must exercise more caution in future.*

Kirsten smirked. 'I was always jealous of you at school. Remember I had those big glasses and I was petrified of speaking to guys?'

'Haha, yeah, I remember. But it hasn't stopped you getting the most gorgeous fiancé.'

Giggling, Kirsten started to undress. 'What happened to you and Marcus? I never heard why you split up.'

'The distance.' Rhona took one last look at her reflection and whipped off her top. Marcus would have averted his eyes if she'd done that in front of him, perhaps muttering how they "got in the way". Laughable really. Silly man. Thank god, they'd split before things went any further. But it left a gap. A lonely place. The companionship had been good. 'I was working in continental Europe and he had a contract in England. It was logistically impossible.' She adjusted her bikini top in the mirror. Maybe it was too revealing, or was that Marcus's silly mutterings again? What if it popped off in the jacuzzi? *Hell.* She tied it tighter.

'That's a shame.'

'It's fine. I'm over it. We weren't exactly crazy about each other. We just rubbed along.'

'After what happened to Fraser and me, I believe when it happens, you'll know.'

'You mean it'll hit me like a bolt of lightning?'

'Pretty much.'

Keeping her back to Kirsten, Rhona shimmied her bikini pants over her hips and curvy bottom, remembering – not for the first time – that buzz she'd experienced when she'd spoken to Calum a few days ago. Just the remnants of the old crush. It had to be that. *Cannot afford to reopen that box. Do not think about it.*

'When did you get the tattoo?' Kirsten eyed Rhona's reflected shoulder in her mirror.

Rhona fixed her hair in a knot atop her head. 'Our whole team got one after I found an ancient piece of pottery shaped like a shell.'

'It's cute.'

'Is it? I'm still not convinced.' Memories of Crete were always accompanied by the knowledge she'd been screwed over.

She and Kirsten stepped out wearing their fluffy robes. Gentle panpipe music floated on the warm air and a delicate fragrance tickled Rhona's nose. 'Looks empty. We've got the whole place to ourselves.'

'The benefits of a Tuesday morning,' Kirsten said. 'It can be a pain working weekends but these kinds of things make it worthwhile. Shall we go in the jacuzzi?'

'Sure.' Rhona hung up her robe and tweaked her bikini straps making sure everything was still in place before lowering herself in. The water bubbled around, instantly calming her. And that aroma. Sea salt? She breathed it in. Perfect bliss. 'We've got a while before the hot stone massage. I don't think I'll move; this is so relaxing.' She lay back her head as the tension left her body.

For several minutes, neither spoke. Rhona soaked in the warmth.

'How's your work?' Kirsten asked.

'Fairly crap.' Rhona dabbed water on her hot cheeks. 'I get emailed pictures to research. It's so dull, worse than being a student.'

'Do you miss the digs?'

'Yes and no. Sometimes they're fun and if everyone gets on, it's a great team feeling. But the last team I worked with wasn't like that. My trench manager, Simon, was lovely and Jay was good fun but that was it. I don't miss the back-breaking work or the dirt.' A sigh escaped her but the bubbles soothed her shoulders. 'I'm kind of at a crossroads. I don't want to go back to that but I'm not sure how to get out. My dad thinks I should go into consultancy but I don't have a lot of experience.'

'Aren't you qualified to do it?'

'I am. Scottish history has always been an interest of mine. I grew up with it and I've always liked to know where it fits in to the rest of the world. I could set up something here but it would take a long time to build a name for myself. There are a lot more qualified people out there, which means I'd either have to charge super low and not make much money or do lots of volunteering until I make a name for myself.'

'Hmm. That doesn't sound great. You should do tours like me; you could focus on archaeology.'

'That's not a bad idea. I've done things like that before, one-off trips to dig sites and the like.' She splayed out her fingers, catching the bubbles between them. 'How's Beth?' Her curiosity about Kirsten's sister cloaked a hidden agenda. Beth was an old school friend of Arran. And Will. And Calum.

'Fine. She's getting married this summer.'

'Ah, yes, Arran's coming home that week so he can go.'

'I'm bridesmaid along with Frank. Well, he's her best man.'

'I remember him, he was always good for a laugh. I take it she's still friends with Will Laird?'

'She's always been good mates with Will.'

'I met him the other day and he took me to a possible-dig site at Kilnarkie. It looks so interesting and it would be something I could do while I was here. I'd love to do it.'

'Then go for it. It sounds ideal.'

'There's no way I can, unfortunately.'

'Why?'

'Because of who owns the land.' Rhona swirled the bubbles.

'Who's that?'

'Calum Matheson.'

'Oh, him.' Kirsten scrunched up her nose. 'He's got quite a reputation.'

'Don't I know it.'

'Beth gets on ok with him, but I guess the history with your family makes it awkward.'

'That's an understatement. My parents would kill me if I got involved.'

'Do you have to tell them?'

Rhona pouted and cogs in her brain leapt into action. 'I suppose not.' It was her life; she could decide for herself. Couldn't she? 'But you know what this island is like. It's not exactly easy to keep secrets.' Her mind chased possibilities and outcomes until she started to overheat. 'I need to get out. I'm too hot now.'

'We should get ready for the hot stones anyway.'

After they were dry, they made their way into the private treatment room. A masseuse welcomed them and Rhona took her position face down on the wonderfully warm pillow. The stones had an instant calming effect and Rhona made up her mind. She wanted to do the dig. That site had a special place in her heart. She'd hung out there as a kid, camped nearby and pretended she was living the life of an Iron Age girl. Part of her soul was still there. If someone else got the contract, how could she sit back and watch them make the finds and take the credit? Like Annike had done. Nope, she couldn't allow it.

Just as she made up her mind, the whole scenario crashed around her, like the poles of her flimsy bivvy had done one time she was camping at Kilnarkie. She and her friends had laughed and propped it back up. But there was no propping up this idea. It wasn't just her parents preventing her. She'd have to approach Calum and volunteer. How could she? He was a man with a vicious temper. And she was determined to exercise more caution in her relationships. Getting involved with a Matheson wasn't a smart play.

She closed her eyes, allowing the warmth to soothe her again.

Once they were fully pampered, they ate lunch and Rhona downed a lot of wine. She hadn't had a day out for months. The last time she'd drank with friends was the beach party in Crete when they'd celebrated finding the shell.

'I think I might approach Calum Matheson about that dig.' She recognised the wine talking but also her heart. 'If I arranged permission over the phone or by email, I wouldn't have to meet him. I could do the dig alone. He wouldn't need to be there.'

'Wouldn't he?'

'Not all the time. Of course, if the excavators turned over something interesting, he'd want to see. And I guess there's a good possibility I might find something.'

'Won't he go crazy if you do? I mean, he probably doesn't want you to find anything, because won't that be expensive?'

'Hmm, maybe.' She took another swig of wine. 'I'm just so curious about what might be there.'

'Then do it. Give a fake name or something and don't tell your parents. Pretend you're helping me with tours or something if they ask where you're going.'

'I expect he'll say no. He hates my family and I don't want to make things any worse.'

'But you'll always regret it if you don't even give yourself a chance.'

'So true.' Rhona pulled out her phone and googled *Calum Matheson*. 'There's an email here for his property business.'

'Go on then. You may as well. If he says no, then so what? It doesn't change much.'

'True.' Except it would cut off the chance of doing something she'd dreamed about since she was a child. *Be prepared.* Because *no* would most likely be his answer. She thumbed out a message and a thrill of wine-charged adrenaline rushed through her as the words flowed. What a rebel! The remnants of the old crush lingered, setting her heart fluttering. This was like sending him an unsigned valentine card; the problem was he'd know exactly who sent it. Well, damn it, if he didn't want her help, he could ignore the message and continue to hate her.

'Right, done.' She smacked her phone onto the table. 'Now, let's forget about it and enjoy our lunch. Tell me about the new house you're building. You don't need an archaeologist too, do you?'

'No. Our planning was passed without any conditions. You should come and see it, though it's a building site just now.'

'I'll borrow Mum's car one day and nip down. That's the problem not having a car here. But it does mean I can drink all afternoon and call Dad's taxi when I'm ready.'

They left the hotel some hours later, Rhona happily tipsy. She hugged Kirsten goodbye twice and almost twisted her ankle as she approached her dad's car. Maybe she'd over-boarded a little on the wine.

'Are you drunk?' Alister frowned and peered at her. His nose twitched like he was sniffing the air.

'Maybe a little. Sorry, Daddy.' She clutched his arm and cuddled him. 'But I do love you. You're the best daddy in the whole wide world.'

'Oh, Rhona, Rhona. What will we do with you? It's time you grew out of this kind of thing and got a job.'

'Yes. That's right. And that's what I'm doing. I'm on it, Daddy.'

He gave her a half-exasperated, half-amused smile and she beamed back.

Chapter Six

Calum

Smoke curled from behind the hedge of the uninspiring semi-detached house. Its steeply pitched grey roof was deeper than the building's low-slung body and two dormer windows sat side by side. The one on the left was Calum's old room. He pulled up in the gravelled parking area, separated from the house by a path and a hedge. Gulls squawked alongside the familiar roar of the car-ferry engines firing up. Calum zapped his 4X4. The ferry times were ingrained in his brain. When he'd lived in this house as a child, he set his watch by them.

If he had his way, he'd take his parents out of here and set them up somewhere a bit grander or at least a bit more private. This little row of ex-council houses was so close to the ferry that all and sundry wandered past in the summer months. But his parents were having none of it. They'd always lived here and they liked it.

Calum tucked his white shirt into the back of his tight jeans and nipped up the verge. In the front garden, the barbecue smoked in the middle of a circle of deckchairs. A little gazebo stood to the left and among the garish bunting was a huge banner reading 'Happy Birthday'. Calum half closed his eyes and flexed his hands before opening the gate. So much for a quiet celebration.

'Happy birthday!'

A pair of arms grabbed him from behind the hedge and dragged him down, clinging around his neck. 'Seriously, Mum.' He stood rigid. 'I can't breathe.'

'Happy birthday to my most gorgeous boy.' She planted a huge kiss on his cheek, then pinched it like he was a toddler. 'You really are the handsomest boy that ever was.'

'Thanks.' He returned her hug briefly. 'I didn't need all this. I thought it was just a barbecue.'

'Would I let one of your birthdays pass without doing something?' She flicked her angular fringe off her face.

'Apparently not.'

'Too right.' She beamed. 'You deserve it. It's a special birthday after all.'

'Since when was thirty-three a special birthday?'

'Since I said so.' She headed towards the house, her bright-yellow dress contrasting with her burgundy hair. 'Ron, where are you?' Anne was a well-known face on the island, not just because of her colourful hair and quirky dress sense, but because she worked in the shop two minutes from their house; often the first and last place on the island people visited. She'd cut down to part-time hours now but Calum expected her to be working there when she hit ninety, she enjoyed it so much.

'There you are, son.' Ron stalked out of the house, his beefy arms and short chunky legs covered in tattoos, shown off by his terrible taste in Bermudas and his wrestler vest. His bald head glinted in the sun as he clapped Calum on the back. 'Happy birthday. You're getting old. Any greys yet? Or have you started wearing a toupee so you don't end up like your old man?' His laugh rumbled.

Calum's lip quirked up. 'So, have you invited people here?' He dreaded the answer. Being alone with his parents would suit him fine, but they loved company.

'Just my friend, Joyce,' Anne said, 'and her husband, Neil.'

'Good.' His shoulders relaxed. They were harmless people. 'I'm having a drink with Will later so I can't stay.' He should have guessed they'd put on a big do.

'Aye, aye,' Ron said. 'Dinnae fret. We won't keep you from your friends but we like to treat you. You've done so much for us.'

Have I? Not that much. They wouldn't let him do more. They were the ones who'd given him the big break in the first place. When Ron's mother died and left them her house, Ron and Anne had turned it over to eighteen-year-old Calum and told him to make the most of it. He had. Or he'd tried. Property could be a gamble but it had brought him success – and stress. No different from any job.

'You look like you need a good dinner.' Anne rested her hands on her hips and scanned him over. 'You can come round any time and I'll make you something if you don't feel up to cooking.'

'Really, Mum, I'm fine.'

They were always so kind. Had he lived up to their expectations? Done them proud? They'd never been able to have any more children. He was their only one. And after he'd let them down so badly as a schoolboy, well... He rubbed his forehead, pushing away those thoughts. He didn't want to put a damper on his birthday treat.

'Take a seat.' Ron pulled out a deckchair and Calum flopped onto it.

'I've made a cordial,' Anne said. 'We'll try it before Joyce arrives. In case it's yucky.'

She bustled back a few moments later, carrying a tray laden with a jug and glasses. Calum raised his eyebrow. 'Very fancy.'

'Probably tastes like piss.' Ron stuck two fingers in his mouth, feigning throwing up.

'Shut it.' Anne eyeballed him. 'You've got a crate load of beer anyway, so it won't matter to you.' She poured a glass and handed it to Calum. He sipped it slowly, bracing himself. It hit his taste buds with a sharp zing.

'Mm, not bad.'

'Good boy.' Anne ruffled his hair like a dog.

Calum stretched on the deckchair, lifting his backside to remove his phone from his pocket.

'I don't know where you got the tall gene from.' Anne shook her head at his legs.

'Probably that bloody postman,' Ron said.

'Oh, wheesht, you.' She flapped at her husband.

Calum smirked into his drink. Bonkers. Both of them. But they were his, and he wouldn't trade them for the world. Both of them were heading for sixty but neither looked it. His mum's bright personality took years off her and Ron worked on boats in the open air, which kept him fit along with the karate. He didn't do that as much these days but he could still pack a mean punch and throw if he had to. 'Are you doing the karate competition this year, Dad?'

'Bugger no. I'm too old for all that jazz. You go knock 'em out, son. Give 'em the old one two for your dad.'

'Yeah. I might enter but I'm out of training.' He used to travel every Saturday to Oban on the mainland for practice. These days his training consisted of pulverising his dummy and occasionally working on throws with another guy on the island.

'Aye, do that, it'll be good for you.' Ron cracked open a can of beer and adjusted a switch on the barbecue.

Calum woke his phone and several new messages blinked. Scanning through them, he dismissed them. 'Honestly, tenants complain about bloody everything. What can I do about a rat in their parking area? I'm not frigging Rentokil.'

Ron chortled, flipping a sizzling burger. A tray of rolls landed on the table next to Calum and he looked up. 'Mum, should I not help you?'

'Absolutely not. Stay where you are. It's your birthday. I insist you relax.'

Calum returned to his messages, ready to switch off his phone when an email caught his eye. He frowned at the sender. Rhona Lamond. That had to be a joke, right? Or some twisted game of Will's? His chest tightened. Will wouldn't be that stupid. But a Lamond message *him*? He tilted the screen away from Ron. No way could his dad read it from that distance, but consorting with a Lamond, even via email, in his parents' garden was weird, like he was doing something illegal.

RhonaLamond21@ymail.com
Dear Mr Matheson,

Mr Matheson? His frown deepened and his pulse sped up – a pounding, nagging beat. No one ever called him Mr Matheson unless they had a complaint or a false accusation. The Lamond MO.

Further to our meeting a few days ago, I would like to put to you a proposal. I have an MA in Archaeology from the University of Edinburgh and have over five years field experience in European archaeology. My knowledge of Scottish history and pre-history in an archaeological context is wide-ranging.

What the hell was this? He scratched at his temple. An application for a professorship? Why was she sending him a CV?

I am currently at a juncture in my career and working on an office-based research project. However, I am looking to get into consultancy work. To do that, I want to gain further relevant experience. If I was contracted to work on the Kilnarkie dig it would be invaluable for my career development. If you were agreeable to my working there, I would be happy to do it at a significantly discounted rate, so it would be beneficial to both of us.

I am of course aware of the unpleasant history between our families, however, as this will be a purely working arrangement, I see no harm in applying thus.

Yours sincerely,

Rhona Lamond

Seriously? Calum switched off his phone and pushed it under his leg. Had he just read that? Was it a joke? It was so ridiculously formal it sounded like she was applying to be lady-in-waiting to the queen.

He glanced up half-expecting Ron to be glowering over him with his hands on his hips warning him never to trust the Lamonds. Or his mother cracking her knuckles and offering to sort them out on his behalf. But Ron was still flipping burgers and whistling to himself and Anne was at the gate chatting to Joyce and Neil who'd just arrived.

Nothing needed done about it immediately and no way was he mentioning it. It could stick to the wall and he'd deal with it when he was back in the office, but he couldn't shake it. It bored into him as he sipped his cordial. Alister Lamond was behind this. He had to be. As well as being Arran's dad, he'd been the teacher from hell at school. Strict and unforgiving. Now he was a sharp and nasty thorn in Calum's side. Was this his latest move in his catalogue of smear campaigns? Get his daughter to work on the project and have her fabricate a whole number of things so Calum would never get the planning consent? It reeked of a set-up.

Joyce parked her large backside onto a deckchair next to Calum and almost toppled it. He leapt up ready to help if things went amiss but she steadied it. He sagged back, letting out a sigh. He didn't fancy hauling her off the ground.

'These things aren't built for people like me,' she said. 'I don't think I'll ever get out of it now I'm in it.'

Calum attempted a smile. Had it registered on his face? His mind was still milling over the Lamonds.

'Happy birthday,' Joyce said.

'Thanks.'

Joyce's husband, Neil, took one of the more practical metal garden chairs and Anne pulled up another one.

'Right, who's for burgers?' Ron scraped one up, balancing it on the end of the flipper and wafting it around like a stocky chef in a tacky street café. 'No need to get up, Joyce, I'll bring them over. Just say what you want in it.'

'Where's your girlfriend today?' Joyce asked. 'I was hoping to meet her at last.'

'What girlfriend?' Calum took a burger on a paper plate from Ron and set it on the low wall surrounding a flower bed.

'Rebekah, is it?' Joyce smiled at Anne who shook her head.

'I told you they split up last year,' Anne said.

'I must have forgotten.'

Calum smoothed his palm down his thigh over his best Italian, velvet-soft denim jeans. 'We weren't really together. We only had a couple of dates.' Why had he let slip to his mum they'd dated at all? Always the wish to be 'normal', but he couldn't deliver. Maybe his mum was right and he was too fussy.

'Pity.' Anne squinted at him. 'I've met her now. She's been into the shop a couple of times with her new boyfriend, Blair.'

Calum clenched his fists. The bunting flapped in the breeze and a soft trail of smoke plumed from the barbecue. He turned away to avoid it going up his nose. Could they talk about something else now?

'Do you know him?' Anne asked Joyce. 'The lad with the blond dreadlocks.'

'Oh, him. Very nice. If I was thirty years younger... Well...' She winked.

Ron sniggered from behind the barbecue.

'Calum missed a trick there,' Anne said.

'I'm right here,' he muttered.

Anne and Joyce gave each other a commiserating look.

'How do you fancy a date with my daughter?' Joyce dusted crumbs from her voluptuous cleavage. 'She's a bit younger than you but she's always between men.'

'I, er... don't think so.'

Anne cocked her head. 'Oh, son. You're such a good boy. I just wish you could be happy.'

'Who said I wasn't?'

'Come on, ladies.' Ron dropped onto a seat, balancing a plate loaded with burgers and sausages. 'Eat up and leave him alone. He's capable of finding himself a girl or two. Aren't you?' Ron flicked him a wink.

'Actually, yes. But right now, I'm perfectly happy on my own.' All true. Casual hook-ups curdled his stomach. So much effort and for what? Where was the connection, the bond... the love? And if love happened slowly, he was down and out. But wasn't it meant to hit you like a cruise liner? His birthday card should read *thirty-three and still waiting*.

After they were stuffed with burgers, Anne brought out a cake decorated like the sea. She'd stuck a toy yacht on top of it and moulded a mini island from green icing. Had he ever had a birthday when she hadn't done something special? Nope. Every time. A truly awesome mum. Warmth surged in his heart. They may not be rich people but they'd always showered him with love. If only he could hug her and tell her how much he appreciated her efforts but no... Closeness even with his parents made him edgy. Even though they might be the only people who found him loveable. He shuddered and his shoulders twitched. Nothing could shake off the unclean feeling. The acne had started it. Then the Arran incident. Now, he was the hated landlord with the bad reputation.

'This is a mini version of your new toy.' Anne waggled the yacht, then kissed his cheek. 'Have you taken her out yet?'

'Only once. I haven't had time. I've been so busy with the properties.'

'Your dad's itching for a go.'

'Anytime.'

'Good lad.' Ron winked at him.

Anne lit the candles and Calum blew them out. Everyone burst into a chorus of 'Happy Birthday'.

Where to look? His neck burned. This was beyond cringy. He forced a smile. Had it worked? When they stopped, he wolfed his slice of cake before getting to his feet.

'Sorry, but I have to go. I'm meeting Will shortly.'

'Aye, for the piss up.' Ron knocked back a swig of beer. 'Off you go then and have one on me.' He stood and shoved a ten-pound note in Calum's pocket.

'I don't need your money, Dad.'

'I insist. Take it and bugger off.'

Anne wrestled Calum into another hug. *Relax and accept it.* But no, his muscles stayed tense. He patted her back stiffly. 'Thanks, Mum. I appreciate all this. It's so good of you.'

'Don't be daft. It's nothing. Just a little something for your special day. And mine. It was thirty-three years ago I got the best present I could have wished for. A beautiful baby boy. I'll never stop being proud of you. You're the best son I could have.'

Even after what he'd done to Arran Lamond, she still believed in him. She always had. When she'd been called to the school after the incident, she'd sat with him, clinging to him, like she was doing now, only shaking. 'It'll be ok. It'll be ok,' she'd said over and over. Numbness froze his blood. Arran's lifeless body was at the bottom of the stairs. Whatever Arran had done, he didn't deserve that. No one did. 'It'll be ok. I'll make sure of it.' But how could she? He'd unleashed a violent monster. Had it left him now or did it lie dormant, waiting to strike another victim another day?

He jumped into his 4x4 and switched on his phone. That loopy message from Rhona Lamond sprang into his head. He tapped his fingertips on the wheel. If she was genuine, it could save him a lot of money. Money? Christ, here he was again, living up to the same old reputation.

But a chance for something else lurked here. He could employ her, watch her like a hawk, save the money, and if she tried to unearth something fake, he'd bring her and the Lamonds to the ground. His hand hovered over the screen.

How to reply? No way was she going anywhere near that site alone. He'd meet her in person. Much easier to gauge her responses. Will said she was nice and nice people were crappy liars. Reading her would be easy. He'd discover if she was genuine or if she was working as Alister's puppet – most likely.

He pulled up the email and typed a quick response.

Dear Miss Lamond,

A dry smirk tugged his lips.

Thank you for your email. Your proposal is interesting but I will need to have a face-to-face discussion with you before I make any commitment. If you could make an appointment to meet me either at the Kilnarkie site or in my office at Tobermory then I would much appreciate it.

Regards,

Calum R. Matheson

Maybe add esquire to the end of his name? Why the ludicrous formality? Was she drunk or on something? As he sped north, he weighed the possibilities. Other people were gullible enough to be taken in but not him. When he'd fully investigated every option, he'd make his decision and not before.

Rhona Lamond. Blonde hair flying in the wind. A lightweight top hugging delicious curves. Blue eyes. Long lashes. A sweet smile. A fire blazed in Calum's belly. 'Jesus, shit'. He scraped his hand through his hair. *Must take care.* Developing a fascination with her was plain crazy. He'd navigated his way past plenty of intelligent, kind and good-looking women over the years, saving them from him and his demons. But inflicting himself on his worst enemy – or his worst enemy's sister – was too low even for Calum Matheson to stoop.

Chapter Seven

Rhona

Rhona sat on her bed, running her palms up and down her jeans. Why the hell had she arranged to meet Calum Matheson? What moment of craziness had seized her? If she'd been sober, she'd never have sent that stupid email. But the dig. Yes, the dig...

'Argh!' She jumped up and held her hand to her forehead. She'd agreed to meet him at the land because she could walk there. If she went to his office at Tobermory, she'd need a lift. How could she hide what she was doing from her parents?

Instead, she'd planned to meet a potentially violent man at a deserted country place. *What kind of idiot am I?* It was Crete all over again. She'd met Annike and they'd house shared. Rhona had helped her out, been kind, friendly and open. What was wrong with that? Wasn't that what people did? But look what had happened. She always tried to assume the best in people. Marcus was a prime example. 'Oh god.' She clutched her face. When would she learn?

Her parents were intelligent; they held the grudge against Calum for a reason. Rhona had seen the damage Calum had done to Arran. She bolted downstairs and pulled open a kitchen drawer. Her fingers closed around the handle of a steak knife. Just in case? No. But her pick would work. It wouldn't be odd to have that with her. She riffled through her backpack on the shelf near the front door and found it. Should she? She sucked her lip for a moment, then stowed the pick in her bag.

Cloudy grey skies loomed overhead and a smir of rain lingered in the air. Rhona nipped into the garden and crossed the lawn towards her mum's studio, craning her neck towards the shore. The tide was out and so low the sandbank spread almost to the other side of the firth with only a narrow channel of sea. 'Hey, Mum.'

'Do you need a lift somewhere? Dad's still out and I'm a bit busy.' She held out her paint-covered hands.

'No, it's ok. I'm going for a walk. I'm heading towards Kilnarkie. If I'm longer than an hour, send a search party.' She kept her tone airy *but please, Mum, remember*.

'It's a bit of a murky day for a walk.' Judy examined her easel. 'So don't be too long.'

'Just a short one.' *I hope*. Rhona shut the studio door and pulled up the hood of her purple waterproof. Her hefty boots clumped along the road and she kept her head bowed as the rain drove into her face. Her ears pricked for the sound of an engine.

Only one road ran in and out. Calum would have to use this way too.

She climbed the gate and strode up the path. The tide was rolling in and waves rushed mournfully against the shore, now some distance away, over the grassy plain. A gull called from high above and Rhona hurried on. She'd crested the hill and was hotfooting it down the almost invisible path when the low grumbling of a car broke the hush. This was it, surely. It had to be Calum. The few scattered holiday cottages were the only nearby habitation. *Help.* They were well out of shouting distance. Rhona slipped her fingers into her bag and found the handle of her pick. She clung to it, ready to whip it out, holding her breath. A dark grey 4X4 came into view. Would he rush by and ignore her?

It slowed and the window came down. Rhona's pulse quadrupled and she edged out the pick. Calum leaned towards the passenger window. 'Do you want a lift?'

'Oh... I, er...' *What now?* Did she get in the car with him? Her heart was drumming like rain on a tin roof. Could he hear it too? 'I'm nearly there.'

'Suit yourself.' He shrugged and pushed the button to close the window. 'You just look a bit wet.'

'Well, ok, thanks.' She had the pick. If he made any sharp moves, she could clobber him over the head with it. Pulling open the door, she jumped in. Her hand trembled as she fumbled for the seatbelt. Did she even need it? It was only a short way over rough ground and she didn't want to let go of the pick handle. What if he did something now?

She edged close to the window, keeping him in her sightline as she clicked the belt. If he made the slightest move, she was ready. He pulled off, rolling the car over the undulating ground.

A deafening ring split the silence and Rhona leapt, bashing her head on the glass.

'Are you ok?' Calum eyed her. The ringing continued.

'Yeah, fine.' Rhona rubbed her temple, keeping one hand firmly on her pick. 'I got a shock. That's loud.'

'I should take it.' Gruline Property displayed on the handsfree screen. Calum grimaced, then jabbed at a button on the dash. 'Hello.'

'Hi.' A man's voice crackled around the car. 'We're still having trouble with the rats. I saw another one at the bins today.'

Calum drummed a steady beat on the wheel with two fingers. 'I've called pest control. They'll be out within the week.'

'When exactly?'

'I don't have an exact date. It's not like they can nip out in a day.'

Rhona silently nodded. Yup. Island life.

'It's not good enough,' the man said. 'We should get a reduction in rent for the inconvenience.'

Calum's jaw went rigid, his knuckles white on the steering wheel. Rhona backed against the window. Was he going to blow a fuse? She fumbled for the door handle. Calum's eyes dulled and his shoulders slumped. An uncomfortable sensation flickered in Rhona's chest. She clenched her fists, fighting an urge to reach out to him. What a drain it must be to have people moaning all the time.

'I can't do that.' His tone was calm but firm. 'Your rent is already very reasonable for that size of house—'

'But it's falling apart. I don't need to remind you about the chimney, do I?'

'No, but that was last year and it's been fixed and you were fully compensated for that. This is a separate issue completely.' He side-eyed Rhona. She blinked and looked at her bag, absently fingering the handle of her pick. *Awkward.* Calum cleared his throat. 'I can't give you a reduction in rent for every inconvenience. It's a house in the countryside, there will be rats from time to time, it doesn't—'

Silence. Calum rammed the button. 'Did he cut me off?'

'Maybe the reception dropped.'

'Yeah. It's not great out here.'

Rhona sucked her lip and glanced at him. He sagged into the backrest and she wasn't sure what to say. Her dad would have no difficulty interpreting the phone call. He'd put it down to Calum being stingy. But it was his job, his business.

He pulled into a quarried area beside the site. Temporary fences had been erected. Were they to protect the site or to stop people like her traipsing up for a nosey?

'How can you stand the stress of your job?' she said. 'That would drive me mad having people calling me about stuff like that.'

He ran his fingers through his dark, neatly trimmed hair. 'Yeah. It can be tough. People think I'm a bottomless pit when it comes to money.' His gaze flicked sideways and he cleared his throat.

Yup. People like my dad.

'Listen.' He faced her square. 'I might as well cut to the quick because there's not much point in anything else.'

'Er, yes.'

'The history between our families will make any kind of working arrangement difficult. It makes me wonder why you want to do this. What are your motives? Did someone put you up to it?' His eyes bored into hers.

Could he read minds just by looking? Because her defences had evaporated. Eye contact lingered. Her grip on the pick became painful. Her heart beat faster. *Deep breath.*

'No, nothing like that.' Her voice came out as barely a whisper. 'I want to investigate this site for my own personal satisfaction. I love it here. It's where I grew up and it's always fascinated me. I hate the idea of someone else getting to do it when I'm right here and I have the skills and the time.' She blinked and let out a sigh. The burn in her chest dulled, throbbing a reminder: *he's a Matheson. I'm a Lamond.* 'But I'm not under any illusions about... the situation.'

'Hmm.' His eyebrows were low, creating an angular quality to his well-proportioned face. Dark hair continued around his jaw in a light stubble.

She swallowed hard, her knuckles still clamped tight to the pick. He rubbed his chin and studied her. Wow. The depth of those eyes, greenish blue, like the surface of the sea on a cool bright day. Were they angry? Or just sad? The hairs on the back of her wrist lifted as his focus shifted away.

Maybe he wouldn't hurt her but he could crush her dreams with one word. His mouth opened and she scrunched her eyelids shut, waiting for the blow. Silence. She opened one eye. What was he waiting for? Just say no and get it over with. Why had she ever thought it would work?

'It's like you said...' she blurted. The silence was too much. 'The history between our families makes this... awkward. When I sent that email, I was...' *Drunk?* Shit, she couldn't say that. It sounded terrible. 'I wasn't thinking straight. I guess I got starry-eyed at the idea of doing a dig here. If there's something waiting to be discovered, I'd love to be the one discovering it, and I'm sure there is.' Why was she rattling on?

'You realise that doesn't sound so appealing to me. The more discoveries you make, the more money it costs me.' He quirked an eyebrow but his expression softened. Rhona's grip on the pick slackened. 'And that's not me being a miser, it's a fact and a practicality.'

'Yes. This is what I have to learn. If I go into consultancy, it's a fine line between keeping the customer happy and doing the job I have to do. That's why I'm prepared to do it on the cheap. All you'd have to pay for would be carbon dating on any finds. My wages would be... Well, nothing.' Her shoulders drooped and her insides followed.

'I'm not that bad. I'd pay you sensibly.' He stared ahead and tapped the steering wheel.

'But...' Did that mean? What did that mean?

'Employing someone from the island will save me money elsewhere. If I hire someone from the mainland, the cost instantly goes up. You're here already and you have the skills. You don't need travel money or lodgings. You sound enthusiastic, but...' He frowned and she clamped her lips shut, not daring to pre-empt what he might be about to say. What was he thinking? He was hard to read. Very subtly, he skimmed over her and tingles erupted in her stomach. The movement was so imperceptible it could easily have been missed or pulled off as casual. Was he silently sizing her up?

'Have you done anything like this before?'

'I've done several digs in Europe and I have an MA in archae—'

'I know. You sent me your CV, remember. But have you ever run an investigation yourself?'

'Not exactly.' She wasn't experienced. God forbid she made a mistake. That would be all he needed to bring her down.

Working for nothing lowered the pressure but the whole thing could be more trouble than it was worth. Had she made a big mistake? 'That's why I'm willing to work for low pay. I need experience and it's so hard to come by. This seems like the perfect opportunity. Or it would be if I wasn't a Lamond and you didn't own the land.'

Their gazes locked and Rhona clung to the pick. Calum adjusted his lapels. The corner of his lips quirked slightly though he still frowned. Rhona let go of the pick, her palm sweaty. She pushed a strand of hair behind her ear, then trailed it under her chin.

'That's the crux of it,' he said.

'So...' She swallowed. 'Should I g—'

'Would you like to look around?' He unclipped his seatbelt but didn't let it go.

'I would, but do you trust me?' Did she trust him?

With a sigh, he released the belt. 'In principle, I trust your offer as genuine.' He toyed with the edge of a gold wristwatch, then tapped it. 'But if I find out this is a trick it will not go well for your career.'

'I swear it isn't.'

With another sweeping glance, his jaw set and he flexed his fingers. 'Ok.' He opened his door and stepped out. Rhona followed, half stumbling over the rocky ground. What was happening? He was letting her do it? Not only would she get to investigate a site she'd loved since she was a child but this could do wonders for her career – her own dig.

'I don't have the plans here.' Calum pulled the collar of his blazer up against the driving rain. 'But the house is roughly positioned around the old bothy.'

'You won't need to survey the whole thing, just the area where the house is going. I see some fascinating ridges over there. It's impossible to tell without digging but that could be the remains of an enclosure or a homestead. Before you do anything, you need a field walk to plot the lie of the land.'

'That'll be your job.' His voice was carried away in the wind.

Rhona pressed her lips together to hold back the smile she desperately wanted to unleash. 'You're letting me do it?'

'Uh-huh.' He pinned his collar to his cheeks. Rain soaked his neat haircut.

Oh my god! She wanted to squeal and dance and sing and throw her arms about him for giving her this chance. Though she wouldn't actually do it. She was a hugger, he definitely wasn't – one look and she could tell. Too stiff.

'Why don't you draw up the necessities, price it and email it to me. I'll check it out against the going rate and see if we can come up with a package that suits both of us,' he said.

'Ok.'

She edged forward and stuck out her hand. His lips curled up; the effect was transformative. Her eyes travelled over the wedge of skin exposed by the open top button of his shirt and she sank her teeth into her lower lip, her heart missing several beats. He slipped his long fingers around hers and a tingle of pleasure leapt up her arm, warming her to the core. She held eye contact, painfully aware she was smiling so widely it probably looked fake. His palm burned against hers. He let go first, squinting into the rain.

'Do you want a lift back?'

'Yes, please. But can you drop me off not too close to the house? I'd prefer if my family didn't know about this.'

'Fine by me. I don't want them to know either. In fact, we should make it part of the deal not to shout about this. I don't want any complications and I'm sorry to say it to your face, but your parents like causing complications for me.'

'Yeah.' Some of the magic ebbed away. Following a lifelong dream she had to keep secret from her family didn't sit right. This was something she wanted to shout from the rooftops, not hide away in her bottom drawer. 'I'll treat it with strict confidence.'

He nodded and they started back to the car. Rhona met his eyes. A flicker of understanding passed between them. This was going to be ok. His arm was a millimetre from hers; the sleeve of his blazer blotched with rain stains, almost brushing against her purple waterproof. The proximity wasn't scary anymore, in fact, it was quite pleasant. How odd to be casually strolling across the machair with Calum Matheson.

Five minutes later, he pulled up on the verge a safe distance from her parents' house. Rhona's stomach fluttered; thoughts darted in and out her head. *I got the job.* The dig was hers. What might she find? And Calum... was, well, an ok guy. Wasn't he?

'I look forward to your email, Miss Lamond.' His eyes glinted and the corner of his lip twitched.

She pressed her fingers to her mouth, barely holding back her giggle. 'You'll be hearing from me, Mr Matheson.'

With a brief wave, he drove off. What he'd been sixteen years ago didn't tally with what he was now. Rhona kept her head down as she went inside. Where she'd been or what she was planning was now her little secret. She darted straight to her room and opened her laptop. She had work to do.

Chapter Eight

Calum

The baby's cries brought a smile to Calum's face. He pressed the phone to his ear and his heart filled to the brim. 'He has a good pair of lungs.'

Sometimes his body was as cold as his lonely soul but Will's chortle broke through the ice, spread down the phone, across the island and warmed Calum to the tips of his fingers.

'Yes, he certainly has,' Will agreed. 'Do you want to come and meet him?'

'Of course, I do.' Calum hopped off his desk and strolled to the door of his office. The trees swayed and branches gusted around, splitting enough to reveal glimpses of the brightly painted village below. 'You just tell me when.'

'I know how busy you are.'

'But this is important, I'll make time.'

'Well, we want to get him out and about so if you're at Kilnarkie, we could take a walk and meet you.'

Calum ran his hand up the back of his neck. Three weeks ago, he'd made the decision to let Rhona work for him and since then he'd filed the relevant paperwork and drawn up her contract. She'd completed her initial field walk and done everything by the book, but something niggled. The fact she was a Lamond, perhaps. But agreeing to keep it quiet from their families implied they had to keep it quiet from everyone. People talked. Mull was a large island but its population was small enough for people to know people who knew people, especially with Calum's mum placed at the centre of the web of information. And Will was a notorious gossip.

'I'm not sure I'll be at Kilnarkie any time soon, so how about I come around to the house? You won't want to walk too far with a new baby. Stick to near the village. Keep him close and I'll come round when you're free.'

'Are you sure?'

'Perfectly.'

'Great. But how come you're not going to Kilnarkie? What's happening there? I spotted an excavator and a Portaloo going along that road. I thought it might be for there.'

Calum closed his eyes and ground his teeth. This was exactly the problem. Will lived on the other side of the bay from Rhona's house. Kilnarkie was further along and round the coast, more exposed to the wild ocean, but it wouldn't stop Will whipping out his binoculars and checking every delivery that went that way. He'd be well aware there was little else there, making the presence of an excavator and a Portaloo highly suspect.

'Who knows what you saw.' Calum paced to his desk. 'It could've been going anywhere. Tomorrow, I have an appointment near you, so how about I drop in about nine? Is that too early?'

'Are you kidding?' Will said. 'If the last few days are anything to go by, nine o'clock is the new four in the afternoon.'

'Likes to get up early, does he?'

'Yeah, he hasn't mastered the art of sleeping for more than an hour at a time yet.'

'That'll keep you on your toes.' Calum rubbed his forehead, checking his online calendar. So much to do. Plus the pile of documents needing filed away. 'Now, I have to go. I'll see you tomorrow and I look forward to meeting baby Angus.'

Calum leafed through the papers on his desk, thumbing the copies of Rhona's certificates, proving she had the credentials for carrying out the work on his land. No point keeping them now. She was a smart woman with all these qualifications. He'd sent details to the local authorities, but he was loathe to discard them completely. Too often he'd ended up having to provide proof of the tiniest details. This time though, when the usual people objected, they could take it up with their own daughter if they didn't think she was qualified enough for the job.

Thoughts like that kept pouncing on him. She seemed genuine, but he couldn't allow her to do anything important alone. When she carried out her watching brief the following day, he'd be there, stuck to her like a shadow.

Stepping up to Will's door, Calum knocked quietly. He didn't want to rap too hard in case Angus was in the middle of one of his short naps.

Will peered around the door, ruddy cheeked and beaming. 'In you come.'

'It's very quiet. Is he asleep?'

'He's just dozed off.'

Morven appeared at the living room door with a tiny blue bundle on her shoulder, her long dark auburn hair swept over the other side. Calum tilted his head. 'Aw.' Where had that sound come from? But the sight was too adorable, Angus's tiny head resting in the crook of his mother's neck. 'He's beautiful.'

'Ah, thanks.' Will clapped his shoulder.

'And how are you, Morven?' Calum asked.

'Knackered.' She stifled a yawn. 'But trying to enjoy it. People keep saying to enjoy these early days because they go too fast.'

'Though they seem very long,' Will said.

Calum nodded. 'My mum always says *the days are long but the years are short.*'

'Probably true.' Morven indicated for them to go into the living room.

'I haven't got you a present yet.' Calum scanned the room. Every inch was covered in balloons, giant cards, teddies, blankets, and unopened clothes in packs and hanging from the drawer fronts. 'I thought I'd find out if there was anything you needed first rather than duplicating.'

'Oh, we've got so much,' Morven said. 'Everyone's been so generous but it'll take forever to sort it out.'

'I've got a card.' Calum fished inside his blazer and pulled it out. 'Probably the same one everyone got you. Mum says she's sold all the baby boy cards and balloons in the shop.'

'Thank you,' Morven said.

Will took the card. 'Calum.' He frowned, though Will never managed to make that look remotely threatening. 'We don't need money.'

'It's not for you. It's for Angus. Put it away somewhere for him and let me know anything else you need or want.'

'This is too generous.'

'It certainly is.' Morven goggled the money.

Calum shrugged it off. 'It's well deserved.'

'I told you already.' Will grinned. 'All we need is a babysitter.'

'Done,' Calum said.

'You're serious?' Will stared at him.

'If that's what you want. Though maybe when he's a bit bigger. He's best with the two of you for now.'

'Brilliant.' Will rubbed his hands together, watching Calum with a raised eyebrow.

'Do you want to hold him?' Morven edged closer.

'Will it wake him up?'

'I don't think so. He seems quite sound. If I put him on you like this, he'll probably stay sleeping.'

Calum stood stock-still as she gently lifted Angus's little body from her shoulder, raised him up and placed him on Calum. The warm weight of him soothed every negative thought and the touch of his little cheek on Calum's neck calmed his pulse rate. 'He's adorable.' Calum curled his palm around Angus's back, holding him firmly but gently, revering him for the precious little human he was. 'You're a beautiful boy,' he whispered. 'Just beautiful. And when I come to babysit, we'll have lots of fun.'

Will furrowed his brow, then grinned. 'There may be trouble ahead.'

'There may indeed.' Calum stroked Angus's back, breathing slowly.

'You need one of your own,' Morven said and Will cleared his throat.

'Maybe I do.' Calum stared out the window. 'But not yet.'

'Er, no,' Will said. 'You're missing a vital part of the equation.'

'Exactly.' Calum circled his palm over the precious little bundle. 'Now, how about I hand him back because sadly I have work to do and much as I'd love to stay for more cuddles, I really can't.'

After he'd said goodbye, he got into his car and sat for a few moments. Cuddling and hugging wasn't him. Not these days. He started the engine and pulled out. His mum kept telling him he'd been the cuddliest boy ever as a child, but he couldn't remember, or maybe he didn't want to. Cuddling little Angus had been a new sensation. Not a bad one, all things considered. Getting to the stage where he could have one himself was like negotiating a thousand-mile obstacle course. He wasn't averse to relationships but he liked to keep them neat – and short. Dates were ok, especially if they involved eating out somewhere smart. Sex was fine, as long as kissing and cuddling were kept to a minimum and that was definitely a problem. Even hard-as-nails women he'd dated liked a lot more cuddling than he was comfortable with. But what the hell could he do about it? Something was always missing. An emotional connection to make him *want* to get close.

He pulled up in the quarried parking spot at Kilnarkie. White clouds drifted high in a blue canopy and the air was warm enough not to need a jacket. Calum had followed Rhona's instructions and worn old clothes, older than usual anyway; he didn't have anything too old. Keeping smart was part of who he was. Still, he'd put on a plain navy t-shirt with his oldest jeans and thick walking boots. He took off the blazer he'd worn for Will's benefit – Will would get suspicious about where he was going if he turned up in anything less than his usual – and stowed it in the boot.

Rhona was already there, chatting to the excavator driver. Her grey t-shirt was tucked into black hipster jeans, which clung to the curve of her bottom. A long ponytail dangled down her back and she flicked it as she chatted. Thoughts scrambled about in Calum's brain, churning out an unexpected mash-up of Rhona holding baby Angus. Wild imaginings of her cradling a tiny baby of her own flooded Calum's brain. It was his baby. Their baby. They'd made it together. *Seriously, what?*

She spun around, spotted him and waved. Now was the time for him to get a grip on himself. Cuddling a baby had sent him on a wander down crazy street. Now he was imagining having babies with the first woman he saw. Projection, right?

Rhona drifted towards him, beaming from ear to ear. She jumped over a rocky patch, her chest bounced and her cheeks glowed pink. Calum's insides burst into flames. The heat spread through his body until sweat broke out on his brow. Did she have any idea what she did to him? Those curves, that face, the hair. Red hot. *Jesus Christ*, if he'd been asked to design his perfect woman… *This, just this.* Her physical attributes, plus her intelligence, her shining smile. Every box ticked except one final one. Surname? Lamond. That box was enough to override all the others.

'Good morning, Mr Matheson.' She glanced up as she reached him with a cheeky grin.

'Miss Lamond.' He folded his arms.

She shoved her hands in her back pockets, thrusting her well-formed chest forward. He swallowed, his jaw tensing. *Eyes on hers. Nowhere else.*

'I'm trying not to get too excited.' She beamed.

'Me too,' Calum muttered. 'Have you started without me? Has something turned up already?'

'No and no. But the anticipation is killing me. I need to stay calm and objective, and now you're here, you can help me.'

'How?'

'By reminding me you don't want to spend too much money.'

'I can do that. So don't go unearthing the sacred remains of St Columba or anything.'

'It won't be anything as dramatic as that.' Her irises sparkled. 'If we're lucky, it might be the foundations and lower walls of some kind of settlement or maybe some fragments or artefacts. But there's always a possibility there might be nothing.'

'Am I bad to hope that?'

'Yes, Mr Matheson, you're very bad.'

The corner of his mouth twitched. 'Sorry.'

She looked away, grinning.

'Not,' he added.

'Let's see who's smiling at the end of the day.'

With all the nonsense fluffing his brain it was easy to forget who he was talking to. His hackles didn't rise at what, a month ago, he'd have considered threatening language.

The excavator driver fired it up and began stripping the top layer of turf. That driver had done a job for Calum before. Hopefully he was oblivious to the Lamond/Matheson feud or hadn't made the connection. Calum side-eyed Rhona. She watched the ground intently, barely blinking as the excavator scraped over the surface. In her arms she clung to a clipboard like it was her new-born child and Calum forced away that thought before babies and Rhona besieged his brain again.

After about twenty minutes, Rhona held up her hand and stopped the driver. Calum's heart rate quickened. Rhona bounded towards the excavator and the driver pulled back. She crouched and pushed soil to one side, then made notes on her clipboard.

'What was that about?' Calum asked when she returned to him.

'Thought I saw something but it was nothing.'

Calum frowned and sucked in his lip. Was there still a possibility this was a set-up? Would she find something for the sake of it? He wanted to believe in her and trust her like she was an impartial individual, but years of ingrained hatred of the Lamonds wouldn't just evaporate.

'This isn't the most exciting job in the world.' Calum scuffed his foot on the grass after they'd stood watching the excavator for goodness knew how long. It groaned forward, creaking and scraping.

'Sorry. This bit is like watching paint dry. Maybe we should take a break. It'll help to focus.' Rhona held up her hand. The excavator engine grumbled to a halt and she shared a few words with the driver before he headed up the hill towards his van. 'He's well prepared,' she said. 'He's got a flask in his van.'

'So do I,' Calum said.

'Really?'

'Of course, Miss Lamond. Have you forgotten what it's like to live here? You can't exactly pop into Starbucks.'

She smiled. 'I know that. I'm just used to doing digs with more facilities.'

'I got you a Portaloo.'

'Such generosity.'

'It bloody is.'

'Thank you.' She patted his bare forearm with her fingertips, her forget-me-not blue eyes trailing upwards until she reached his face. Calum went rigid. Instinct nudged him to back off but he didn't. The energy burning low in his gut forced him to stay put. Because he wanted to get closer. Her touch was shaking up the status quo in his nerve ends. His breathing quickened and he cleared his throat.

'Do you want to share some tea? I might have a spare cup.' He edged away.

'Go on then.'

He nipped back to the car and dug around in the boot. What was happening to him? Why these sudden urges and bizarre thoughts?

'I'm still hopeful,' Rhona said.

Calum jerked up, almost knocking his head. *She followed me.* 'About what? Hopeful that we don't find anything?'

'Yes, of course, cheeky.'

'Hmm.' He poured a cup of tea into a plastic mug and passed it to her, taking care not to touch her. Too risky.

'How come you have all this stuff in your car?'

'Because this is my mobile office. I have properties all over the island. From Fionnphort to Tobermory and in between.'

'And you've never had archaeological conditions before?'

'This is my first new build.' He perched on the edge of the boot, bringing him eye level with her chest. *Shit*. First mistake. He dropped his gaze to the swirling liquid in his cup. 'Most of my properties have just needed general upgrades. The one at Fionnphort was an extension and no conditions were attached other than the aesthetics had to be in keeping with the area.'

'I think it'll become more and more a thing here.' Rhona sipped her tea. 'So little archaeology work has been done on this island.'

'I still don't share your enthusiasm, sorry.'

'Don't you care about who might have lived here in the past?'

'Not really.'

She snorted. 'At least you're honest, but I can't imagine that mindset. You want to build a home here. People's lives are going to unfold inside it. Imagine unearthing a story of someone else's life. People whose stories have been buried for thousands of years. Imagine finding even one clue as to how they lived.'

'I don't think my imagination works like that. I tend to imagine things in the future rather than the past.'

She flashed him a smile. 'I'm going to convert you.'

'Good luck with that.' He raised his mug. 'Just make sure it doesn't cost me any more money.'

Calum checked his watch – almost three o'clock. The tension in his shoulders ebbed. Nothing of note had turned up. He glanced at Rhona. Her head hung to the side, her hands slung in her pockets. Her bounce had deflated, or was she concentrating?

A few minutes later, she held up her hand again, and the driver backed off. Crouching, she scrabbled around in the dirt. Calum approached, folding his arms, a frown growing. His shadow crossed where Rhona was combing the ground and she squinted up. 'You're not going to like this.'

'You've found something?'

'It might not be anything significant, an old farm wall perhaps, but I have to investigate it.'

Calum sucked in his lips and rubbed his chin. So this was it.

'Look.' She beckoned him. He stooped and peered over her shoulder. 'You have to get right in.'

He shuffled in beside her, resting his backside on his heels. His bare arm a hair's breadth from hers. The heat from her skin was palpable. She pointed into the soil at a ridge. 'This is a solid line and it's man-made. Do you see here?'

'Kind of, but it doesn't look like anything to me.'

'That's why I have to dig. Then I can investigate it. You'll need to call off the excavator for today. This is a hand job.'

'A what?'

'Shit, sorry, that sounded wrong, didn't it?' She screwed up her face.

Calum covered his eyes and shook his head, then slowly drew his fingers around his jaw. 'Ok, I'll tell the driver he can go.' He made to get up but stumbled over an uneven patch of overturned soil and fell onto his backside. 'Bugger.' He leapt to his feet, dusting the mud from his rear.

Rhona smirked. 'I told you to wear old stuff.'

'I did.' He tapped on the excavator door and spoke to the driver before returning to Rhona, who was on her hands and knees. Her relationship with dirt was almost intimate.

'Look at this.' Her voice chimed with excitement. 'It might be the remains of a hearth. I really hope it is.'

'Why?' Calum crouched beside her again.

'Because the hearth is the heart of a home. This could be a homestead of people from hundreds, possibly thousands, of years ago. People who looked out on this same landscape but used it so differently.'

'Keep trying. I'm not with you yet.'

She twisted around and sat cross-legged like a schoolkid, resting her elbows on her knees. 'You're hopeless.' Her gaze travelled from his face, down his bare arms and towards his backside. 'And you have a dirty butt.'

'Ok, that's just a cheap point.' He stretched around, rubbing at the seat of his jeans.

Rhona giggled and leaned towards him. He froze. Was she about to butt him over with her head? Nope. Worse. She rested her forehead on his shoulder for a second and laughed. The earthy aroma of her hair, mingled with floral conditioner caught him deep. 'Sorry.' She peeked up. 'This is just such an amazing discovery.'

'What is?' He stumbled again, trying to get away. 'This wall thing or the mud on my backside?'

She smirked and glimpsed back at it. 'Do you want me to wipe it off for you?' Her tone was teasing, but the thought of her attempting it made him leap to his feet.

'No, I don't.'

Rhona rocked onto her knees again and put her hands on the ground, examining the soil, still giggling and shaking her head.

Was she laughing at him? Like she used to at school? She hadn't been the only one. Her brother, his supposed best pal, had laughed himself silly at Calum's acne and his refusal to join sports clubs.

'You'll never get a girlfriend, mate,' Arran had teased. 'Not with those craters on your face. Except maybe Hannah McDonald.' He puffed out his cheeks and chunked out his arms.

'Hannah's ok.' Calum's neck had burned.

'No way.' Arran almost fell to the ground laughing. 'You like big Hannah.'

'Why not?' She was bright, cheery, kind. So what if she wasn't stick thin and plastered in make-up?

Maybe she would have dated him but Calum didn't get the chance to find out. Arran asked her out and made a big deal of snogging her in front of Calum whenever he could. Arran's motives were suspect, but Hannah seemed happy so Calum didn't say anything... at first. Sneaking away to the mainland for karate on Saturdays was his escape. He couldn't face the football team or the golf club with Arran stalking around like a peacock.

'Calum.' Rhona was watching him. 'I'm sorry. That was totally unprofessional. It's just with you being you.'

'What do you mean?'

'Well, I feel like I know you because... You were my brother's friend.' Her voice trailed off and her thick eyelashes fluttered. 'Though technically I don't know you at all. So, I shouldn't be laughing at your... butt.'

'Right.'

'Because it's actually quite a nice butt.'

'You're making it worse.'

She dragged her fingertips down her cheeks. 'I really am, aren't I?'

'Yes.' He nodded, 'And you've just covered your face in mud. Now you look like one of your prehistoric people getting ready for battle.'

'Ha! I've always been a dirty girl.'

'You sure have a way with words, don't you?'

'No. That's your filthy mind, not me.'

'Hardly.'

'It's the only filthy bit about you. You're way too clean for an island guy.'

Calum adjusted his watch. 'Being messy isn't a stipulation for living here.'

'It should be. That's another mission for me.'

'What? To get me down and dirty?'

Her eyes nearly popped out. *Shit, shit, shit, you idiot.* What was he doing? Letting his mouth enter into her flirtatious chit-chat.

'Now who's got the way with words? Really, Mr Matheson, I'm shocked.'

'Indeed.'

'But if you're looking for someone to show you a good time in the mud, you've found the right girl.'

'I'll bear that in mind.' He wrapped his arms about himself, gazing out to the rolling sea. A gust of wind ruffled his short hair. 'But not today. Right now, I'm leaving you to your mud pit.' Yup, he had to get far away from her.

'Ok.'

'Just don't go digging up anything too expensive.'

'Aye, aye, Captain Matheson.' She raised two fingers to her forehead.

Calum strode back to his car, jumped in and flung his head back into the rest. *Shit, shit, shit... shit.* What the hell was going on? The explosion in his chest should be because his project just got a lot more complicated, but it wasn't. His body throbbed with unanswered need and he squirmed in his seat. She was good company. More than. He was drawn to her. *No. No. No. Bottle it.* Developing feelings for Rhona Lamond thrust against every boundary he'd constructed in the last sixteen years. Sensible Calum had to screw his head back on and stick to business.

Chapter Nine

Rhona

Using a Portaloo on a daily basis wasn't what Rhona had envisaged for her return to Mull. Neither was sneaking around, avoiding her parents so she didn't have to explain why she was covered in mud. Judy spent a lot of time closeted in her studio and Alister often took himself off to fish; Rhona tried to time her returns with them being out the house. The one time Judy had quizzed her about her muddy clothes, Rhona told her she was helping a friend with gardening.

Lying, even by omission, felt wrong, but if she confessed now, they'd flip. Even saying the word Matheson triggered raised voices and angry words. Finding out she was working with one would tip them over. They'd start a witch-hunt, demanding Calum was publicly flogged, and forbid her going near Kilnarkie. She couldn't allow that. Not since discovering the wall they'd unearthed contained the remains of what she surmised to be an Iron Age hearth.

She'd bagged several samples and sent them for carbon dating, then emailed photographs to Simon. He'd sent back some words of encouragement, pleased she'd got involved in such a project.

If only she could share it with her parents. She might not be pulling in as much money as her siblings but she was making discoveries, and important ones too. Surrounded by her tools, she sat in her muddy ditch gently picking off more layers of dirt. This was no better than anywhere else she'd worked but it was hers. The responsibility was all new to her.

'Morning.' Calum was striding towards her, adjusting his gold wristwatch. This made up for the drudge work. Her mood lifted and her senses tingled as he got closer. She could forgive his complete lack of interest in anything historical because she enjoyed talking to him.

'Hi.' Her gaze connected with his and her tummy swooped. He was in a dark navy t-shirt again and it fitted well around shapely pecs and nicely formed biceps. No words passed between them but their eyes made out, overloading her system with bolts of electricity. Did he know what was happening inside her? Did he sense it too? How could he not?

He blinked and unfolded a navy cushion pad, laying on the edge of the trench.

'Seriously?' Rhona frowned, getting to her feet. 'You have a cushion? Is that to protect your delicate rear?'

'No, it's to protect my designer jeans.' He plonked himself on top of it. 'Now, how's it going today? Has anything else turned up?'

Rhona dusted her hands together, then did her knees. A lost cause. 'I'm clearing out the wall. Once I've exposed as much as I can,' – she shook flecks of soil from the neck of her t-shirt – 'I'll examine the hearth.'

'Ok.' Calum's focus flickered over her chest.

She folded her arms. *Only the wall!* She wasn't exposing herself. Her skin tingled under her t-shirt and it was nothing to do with the soil particles. Their gazes locked again, moving in sync from eyes to lips and back. *Oh god, yes.* He could do whatever he wanted. She ran her fingers along her collarbone.

'So…' Calum cleared his throat. 'Can I ask you something?'

'Sure.' She parked herself beside him, dangling her legs into the trench while his feet almost touched the bottom. The skin on her upper arm tugged like it was trying to drag her closer and attach itself to him.

'Once you've unearthed everything within the proposed house boundaries. What happens then? Will I ever be allowed to build here?'

'Probably. Unless something turns up on the scale of Skara Brae or Stonehenge, you'll be fine. But that's why everything has to be fully recorded. Much as we'd like to, archaeologists can't prevent people building on the past. Look at all the digs taking place in cities with Roman remains. Our job is to salvage what we can and keep accurate and detailed records of the contexts and the parts that can't be removed or saved. Like this wall. Once I've detailed it and the report has been published, it's highly unlikely it'll prevent you from building. But it needs to be investigated just in case. There could be anything lurking down here.'

'Have you ever found anything significant? Anywhere?'

A cool breeze stole the heat from her neck. 'I found a lot of artefacts when I worked in Crete. Some more significant than others. My best find was a shell made from pottery. It was really unusual and rare.'

'Wow.'

'Yeah. I can show you photos on my phone but my hands are a bit messy. That was my last dig.' She sighed and picked at a nail.

'Sounds like you miss it.'

'That dig wasn't great. The team didn't gel and one woman stole my work and got a promotion on the back of it. So, I don't have fond memories of it.'

'That's dreadful.'

'Yup. I miss Simon though.'

'Is that your boyfriend?' Calum shifted on his cushion.

'No. Simon was my trench manager. I loved him, he was so kind.'

'Sounds like he *should* have been your boyfriend.'

'He's a sixty-year-old married man, so I don't think so. He was like a kind uncle.'

'Well, now you've got a thirty-three-year-old grumpy bastard as a manager, so things are surely looking up.'

'They definitely are.' She leaned into him with a playful bump and her body inflated at the touch. His jaw set and his upper body froze. *Oops.* He always shied away from physical contact. Because she was a Lamond? Or he thought her over-friendly? Not everyone was as touchy-feely as her, but she hadn't missed the look in his eyes earlier. 'I'm failing in both my missions though. Especially the mud-related one. This cushion is not acceptable, Mr Matheson.'

'Tough. Because wherever I go, it goes too.'

'I'll find a way of getting it.' She waggled her eyebrows.

'Some of the stuff you come out with is bordering on suggestive and edging towards inappropriate.' His brows met in the middle. So severe. He hadn't been like that since the first day.

She clamped her hands to her mouth. 'Oh my god, I'm so sorry.'

The corner of his lips quirked up. 'Had you worried there, no? Did you think I was about to officially reprimand you, Miss Lamond?'

'Don't joke. I should be sensible.' She hopped into the trench.

'Sounds like a lost cause.' He shook his head, looking towards the muddy wall. 'So, you still haven't found any papyrus drawings of the family who used to live here or some buried scrolls with instructions on how to find the Holy Grail?'

'Easy, Indiana. This job never gets that exciting in real life.'

'Did you expect daring adventures when you went into it?'

'No. Nothing like. I've always been curious about the past. I walked over this land hundreds of times as a child. I used to play games that I was someone living thousands of years ago. I often went to the ruined churchyard with my three besties and we put up a bivvy and camped out.'

'A what?'

'Like a tent made from tarps propped on sticks.'

'Are you mental?'

She shrugged. 'Probably. But that's why I was so keen to do this job. This place is in me. It's been part of my life for a long time.'

'I can't believe you camped out like that. Did you sleep in it?'

'Kind of. We were kids, so we talked most of the time. It was brilliant.'

'Weren't you freezing?'

'Only the time it fell down.'

'Good god.' He pinched the bridge of his nose and his watch gleamed on his beautifully formed forearms.

'Haven't you ever been camping before?'

'No. We once toured in a campervan but that was it.'

'You haven't lived. It's an awesome way to become one with the environment.'

'Why would I want to?'

'You are hopeless.'

'I tried to warn you.'

She smirked. 'I thought archaeology would be like coming face to face with the past and experiencing it first-hand but it's mostly either mud or computers. One extreme to the other. I do love it, but it's like a glorified hobby sometimes. The pay is rubbish, no offence.'

'None taken. All my employees complain about that but I'm not made of money.'

'My parents think you're loaded.'

'Half the people on this island think that. I do have money and I am fortunate but it's not endless and I've worked for it.'

'I know you work hard. I wouldn't want your job for any money.' Rhona leaned over and patted his knee, before kneeling on the mucky ground. 'So, your bucket list just got longer. Now, it's to get you to like history, to get you mucky and to get you to sleep in a bivvy.'

'That's your bucket list, not mine.'

'Seriously? You think my bucket list is to give you a history lesson, then do dirty stuff before sleeping with you in a tent?' She screwed up her lips, struggling to keep her face straight.

Calum put his hand over his mouth, his shoulders shaking with suppressed laughter. 'You are awful.' He steepled his fingers, pointing them at her. 'Really awful.'

'Sorry not sorry.'

He got to his feet and carefully picked a path through the mud to where she was kneeling. 'So, what is your real bucket list? To find a golden mummy in the Valley of the Kings or something?'

'Not really.' She grabbed her trowel and scraped at the wall. 'I would love to go to Egypt for a holiday but I've already travelled so much for work. Doing this dig is fulfilling one of my dreams. Another thing I've always wanted to do is hire a boat and travel around the islands to see how they connect by sea. That was much more common in the past than it is now and I'd love to experience it myself.'

'I've got a boat,' he said.

'You don't, do you?' She knelt up level with his crotch and he inched back.

'Yes. I do. But I'm not letting you loose with it. Though I might take you if you ask nicely.'

'Get stuffed. I might be on my knees but I'm not begging a Matheson for any favours.'

'Nicely put, Miss Lamond.'

She pout-smiled at him.

'But I'm joking.' He flicked back his hair. 'I would take you... If you wanted.'

'Really?' She cocked her head and he nodded. 'I'd like it if you were with me.'

'I think I'd—' He stopped and spun around. Voices. Rhona sat up tall. She'd heard them too. Someone shouted Calum's name in the distance.

'Oh shit.' Calum balled his fists, his gaze flicking from side to side. 'What's he doing here?'

'Is that Will?'

'Shit, yes.' Calum vaulted out of the trench and paced towards Will. Rhona peeked over the edge. A young woman with a baby-carrier strapped to her front was strolling along with him. Calum had turned on the charm and he gesticulated around the far side of the site, drawing their focus away from the dig. He patted the back of the baby-carrier and both Will and the woman smiled.

Rhona frowned as the woman unstrapped it carefully and lifted out a little blue bundle. *Aww.* She handed him to Calum. *What?* He cradled the baby and gently stroked his cheek. Rhona's ovaries burst into life. Her heart fluttered like butterflies were racing inside. Calum looked powerful without being bodybuilderish and the baby was so tiny in comparison. But seeing that wee head nestled in the crook of his elbow was melting her knickers.

What the hell was she thinking? Having a child to unite the warring Matheson and Lamond clans? Mental! She'd gone from playing out a teenage crush to wanting babies with Calum in zero to sixty seconds. *No, no, no. Hormones... get back into place! Now!* But whatever it was about him that appealed to her on the most visceral level, she couldn't shake it.

Chapter Ten

Calum

Angus was like a soothing heat pack, keeping Calum calm. Calmer than any t'ai chi practises he'd tried over the years. If he was annoyed with Will for nosing into his business, no one needed to know. All that mattered was that he kept cuddling this little guy.

'So, where are you off to now?' He focused on the little blue bundle cradled in his arm. Angus let out a gurgle.

'Here.' Will bounced on his toes. 'We came to see what was happening.'

'I just told you.'

'You didn't explain why Rhona Lamond was kneeling in a ditch at your feet.'

Calum's jaw stiffened. He forced himself to breathe in tandem with baby Angus and smiled at him.

'Will, that's a really crude way of putting it.' Morven placed her hands on her hips.

'Yeah, sorry.' Will's cheeks reddened and he smirked at Morven. 'But you thought it looked suspect too.'

'No, I didn't.' Morven's eyes flashed towards him then Calum.

Calum raised Angus to his shoulder, inhaling the cotton fresh wash-powder scent from his all-in-one suit. 'Clearly you're both suffering from lack of sleep. Now, let's get Angus back to you, Morven.' He kissed Angus's cheek, patted his back, then passed him over. Morven manoeuvred him into the carrier, keeping her gaze low.

'So, what *is* going on?' Will asked.

'Rhona's working for me.'

Will raised an eyebrow. 'How did that come about? You were dead against the idea.'

'The situation's changed.'

'Indeed.' Will packed the word full of speculation. 'I see.'

'I'm quite sure you don't.' Calum ran his hand up the back of his neck. 'Business is business. But for everyone's sake it's best if we don't shout about her being here.'

'I won't say a word,' Morven said.

'Me neither.' Will flicked Calum a wink.

Calum glared at his friend. 'Make sure you don't.'

'Has she found anything?' Will asked.

'She's made a few discoveries, yes.'

'Can we look? Archaeology fascinates me.'

'Go ahead. You'll make her day. She's desperate to make me a history lover but it's not happening.'

'Sounds very chummy.' Will smirked.

Was there any point in replying? Will had clearly formed his own idea about what was going on and after the flirting, what could he say? *What's got into me?* He didn't flirt – nope – not him. If he liked someone, he wasn't afraid to ask them out, but flirting? No. But with Rhona it was almost natural. Fun. Yes, fun. *Having fun with a Lamond?* What was the world coming to?

They made their way over to the trench and Rhona peered up; her brow furrowed and her focus flickered between Calum and Will. Calum held his thumb and forefinger together forming the ok sign behind Will's back.

'Hello.' Will leaned over the trench edge. 'Am I allowed in here?'

'Sure,' Rhona said.

'I don't have to mind my feet, do I?'

'Only if you love mud as much as Calum.'

'Funny,' Calum muttered.

Will jumped into the trench. 'He's a terrible clean freak.'

'Yes, it's disgusting having a liking for being clean.' Calum folded his arms. 'Revolting, in fact.'

'Shall I help you down?' Will asked Morven.

'No, I might get stuck.'

'This is my wife, Morven. And our son, Angus.' He beamed at Rhona.

'Nice to meet you.' Rhona gave Morven a wave. 'I'd love a cuddle of the wee cutie but I'm way too mucky.'

'Eh, where's my sitting pad?' Calum glared at Rhona, setting his fists on his hips.

'No idea.' Her lashes fluttered and she waggled an eyebrow. Flames licked his insides, waking a sleeping tiger. *Christ.* He wanted to rip off his shirt, pull her close and kiss her until his breath ran out. Mud and all.

'Seriously?' He gritted his teeth and a low growl rumbled at the back of his throat.

'You had a cushion out here?' Will barely hid his glee.

Calum scanned the ground. 'It was not a cushion.'

'No, it was a pad for his very clean bottom.' Rhona giggled.

'Oh, ha bloody ha.' Calum narrowed his eyes. Teasing usually set him on edge. But the emerging tiger didn't care. It wanted to ravish Rhona.

'Oh, Calum. I'm joking.' Rhona stepped up beside him and prodded his side. 'I love you really.'

What did she say? His brain was still processing the words when she ducked down and pulled out his rolled-up sitting pad from behind a pile of turf.

'There's your pillow. Now you can keep your bottom nice and clean.'

Calum took the kneeling pad from Rhona, not making eye contact with Will or Morven. Glances laden with meaning and intrigue were being exchanged, burning like a hot rod on his back. Rhona beckoned Will to the wall, like nothing odd had escaped her lips, and started to explain what she'd uncovered so far. Calum lay the pad down and shoved his hands into his pockets. How could he get away from here without looking rude or guilty of some unknown crime?

'Do you allow volunteers on digs?' Will asked.

'Yes,' Rhona said. 'Sometimes. If it's a community dig then definitely but with this kind of commercial dig, it's not really appropriate.'

Calum raised his eyebrows. She'd finally decided something needed to be appropriate, had she? A bit late in the day for that.

'I'd love to help with something like that,' Will said. 'Though it's not practical just now.'

'You spend time with your baby. That's the most important thing.' Rhona smiled, waving to summon him closer.

Will bent over, examining the finer details. Rhona prodded her finger in the soil. Calum checked around. Was Morven ok? She was ambling down the hill to where the grass sloped to a white sandy shore.

Will and Rhona's interactions were perfectly normal. But a swell of irritation bubbled in Calum's gut. Why didn't Morven come back and call Will away? Surely he was too close to another woman not to annoy her? Rhona laughed and waved wildly as she explained something. *That should be me.* Why hadn't he listened or cared? He wanted to coax that joy from her; it shouldn't be Will.

Because this is work. Just work.

Screw work. He almost said the words aloud, words no one would believe he could utter. But he had to face facts. He liked Rhona for Rhona. She lit the touchpaper on his skin and sent a fire to his soul. For all he hated touching and contact, right now, he wanted nothing else but to hold her in his arms.

What was she doing? She leaned over, pointing at something. *That top... Shit.* Will was getting an eyeful. *How can he find that bloody wall more interesting? Jesus Christ.* Calum loosened his collar and cleared his throat. 'Will, I think Morven wants to head home, she's pacing over there.'

'Oh, right.' Will straightened up. 'Yes, we should start walking back. But I'd love to come another time and see how this is getting on.'

'Any time you like,' Rhona said. 'This'll take at least a week, maybe more. It's impossible to put a time on it.'

'Or a price,' Calum muttered.

'Thank you.' Will waved as he headed towards Morven.

Calum vaulted out of the ditch and fell in step with Will. 'Remember, don't you go blabbing about her working here.'

'I won't.' Will tapped his nose. 'I'm glad to see you're trying to mend the feud.'

'That's not what I'm doing.' Mending things with the Lamonds was a step too far. 'She's getting paid to be here and I'm saving myself the difficulties of hiring an outside contractor. At the end of the job, we part company and that's that.' Good god, he sure could spout the shit. How could he listen to himself?

'Aye, business as usual,' Will said.

'Exactly.'

'Same way you like your women.'

'Meaning what?'

'Does the job, then off she trots.'

'Shut up.' Was that what people thought? True, he didn't do long-term relationships but that wasn't because he enjoyed casual flings – far from it. He hated one-night stands or intimacy with people he didn't know but he didn't dare attempt longer relationships. Who'd have him once they discovered what lurked inside him?

'Just don't do that with this one. She's too nice for that.'

'Do what? There's nothing going on here.' *Another lie.* Plenty was going on, if only in his mind, but he was on a roll. 'Stop trying to see things that aren't there.'

'Wouldn't dream of it.' Will poked his tongue into his cheek.

'Good.'

Will took Morven's hand and Calum waved them off. Once he was sure they were out of earshot and sight, he scooted back to Rhona, hopped into the trench and crouched beside her.

She scratched at the ground with her pick, her nails black. 'Do you think they'll blab?'

'They better not.'

She stopped scraping and met Calum's gaze. 'I do feel a bit bad not telling people.'

'Hopefully it won't be for much longer.' An ache swelled in his chest. Part of him didn't want to say goodbye to Rhona, the same part that wanted to draw her close, extra close. But he had to, of course he did. She was a Lamond and always would be. No getting round it.

She glanced back at the soil with a faint trace of a smile.

'What were you telling Will?' he asked.

'Nothing that'll interest you.'

'Try me.' His hand hung on his knee close to her. Touch her arm? Could he? Should he?

'I already have.'

'Try again. Please.' He flexed his fingers.

Her lips curled up, dimpling her rosy cheeks and the glint returned to her cornflower blue eyes. Carefully, she laid down her trowel and swept a strand of hair behind each ear, opening a curtain on her beautiful face, and smearing mud across it. 'I was showing him the remains of the hearth. Seeing it makes it real. I can see the people and sense their lives like they're still here. A couple starting out, building a home and making it their own.' She stopped talking and the scene seemed to play in her bright irises. 'It was very gender defined back then. She was out gathering. He was fishing. But they were both building and creating their home. When darkness fell, they were together, keeping warm.' Her cheeks tinged a deeper shade of pink than usual and she dragged a finger through the muddy pit she'd dug, tracing what looked like a heart shape. 'It's all romantic nonsense. Those days were like living in a developing country with the constant threat of war, poverty and barbarism.'

Calum pulled a face. 'I liked your first image better.'

'Exactly. Softening the reality works wonders. They were highly skilled people. They built, carved, wove, made metalwork, so it wasn't all bad. But it would have been harsh. Summers here are warm enough but the other seasons would have been as wet and windy as they are now.'

'And that's the life you wanted to recreate in your bivvy?'

'Yes, but only for a night here and there – with plenty of blankets.'

'You have some funny ideas.'

'Oh, come on. Even you must see the appeal of this spot.'

'I do. That's why I bought it.'

'Are *you* going to live here?' Her eyes grew even wider.

He dragged his hand down the back of his neck and drew in his lips. 'I don't know. I thought about it. But I'm not sure. I'm working on a project with a friend to provide affordable housing for locals.'

Rebekah. The friend he'd met last year and they'd fallen into a safe friendship. He'd quickly given up on chasing anything else. On paper, she seemed perfect. If anyone could have forgiven his history, it was her. She understood what it was like to fight demons from the past. But she was better with Blair. Anyone who saw them could work that out for themselves. When it ended, bitterness had seeped in, resentment maybe. But now he was cool about it. She hadn't set an all-consuming fire raging in his gut... like the one kindling right now.

He cleared his throat. 'Land for sale on Mull is limited and not always suitable. This is a big plot and I was considering donating it to the project. But I suspect that's not feasible now. It's so remote and I'd have to reapply for planning permission, which would by no means be guaranteed, and now you've unearthed this, there's every likelihood more treasures are waiting to be discovered.'

'You got that right.' Rhona wiped her palms on her jeans. 'I didn't know you were involved in community projects.'

'I don't shout about it.' Of course, she was surprised. Her parents painted him as a monster, so the poison would be through their daughter.

She drew up her shoulders as if she was cold, then wrapped her arms around herself. The urge to hold her bit into him again, pushing him closer to her. How did she manage to smell so captivating covered from head to foot in mud? The light floral aroma suited her to a T. She was a summer garden personified.

'It's great you're involved with things like that,' she said. 'Such a thoughtful thing to do. But I agree, this land isn't right. You'll definitely get conditions again even if your planning permission is granted in principle. So why not build the house you planned here and live in it? It's perfect.'

'Yeah.' What a lovely thought.

She swept away a stray curl from her cheek. If they could sweep away the family history as easily, he'd ask her out, and take things from there. Maybe things would develop, they'd get serious, build this house together and recreate a modern version of her Iron Age fantasy. His parents' faces swam before him. *Jeez, what am I thinking?* What about the anguish it would cause Rhona if her parents disowned her? How could they live in a house just over a mile away with that amount of bad feeling? It wasn't possible or fair. And after what he'd done to her brother, she was the last woman on earth he could inflict himself on.

His fantasy fizzled out in the depths of her eyes. How carried away could he get? Even with Rhona out of the equation, the problem of the Lamonds living so close was off-putting enough. It was the main factor preventing him from moving forward on the build. The dream house wouldn't be the same with them so close.

'I know what you're thinking,' she said.

'Do you?' Could she? Was his body giving off raw signals? Ones her close-to-nature, Iron Age people might easily interpret?

'Yup. You like the idea of living here, but you're not so keen on certain people in the neighbourhood.'

'Uh-huh.' He rubbed at his forehead. 'Bang on, exactly that.'

'Thought so. I should get on, you know. I don't want my boss thinking I'm a slacker.'

'I'm sure he doesn't think that.' Calum flicked her a little wink and she grinned.

'I wouldn't like to chance it.'

'Ok.' His fingers twitched, then he reached out and gently patted her upper arm. Initiating intimacy was something he never did but the urge to touch her was burning a hole into his soul. She put her hand over his and stroked it for a few seconds, then, letting go, she returned to her place on the ground. His heart roared with loss of contact.

'Your visits make my day.' Her voice was barely a whisper like she didn't really want him to hear.

He pretended he hadn't, it made things simpler, but what? She meant that? He made her day. Did she know she made his too? He'd spent way more time here over the past week than was necessary, neglecting his other jobs.

'Bye for now,' he said.

The dirt she'd transferred to the back of his hand was still there when he got to the car. He hadn't even considered washing it off as he passed the Portaloo; in fact, cleanliness be damned, he might never wash it ever again.

Chapter Eleven

Rhona

The following day, rain slammed down, pooling in the trench. Rhona's boots sank as she dragged her way across. This was too much – even for her. Trudging back towards her house, she thumbed out a message.

RHONA: Not able to work today. There's too much water and mud in the trench. Sorry X

At least she'd tried. She'd had a pointless walk in the rain anyway. When she got back to the house, she had a reply.

CALUM: I never thought you'd ever say the phrase too much mud! But no worries. Take care.

With every site visit tension simmered. Not the he's-a-Matheson-so-I-hate-him tension she got if she mentioned his name at home. A much more pleasant tension. One that kept her awake at night thinking about him.

She hung her sodden waterproofs in the front porch, her mind popping back to their school days when she'd dreamed of being the one to melt him. That could almost be notched up as an achievement now. Maybe he hadn't melted completely but he'd definitely softened. Their new reality addled her head... He was her employer and her family's arch-enemy but also someone she found attractive. What did she really want from him? Her heart and body were on a different page from her brain – sending her confusing messages.

Nelson, the huge fluffy grey cat, stalked down the hallway and jumped on the sofa, making the only noise in the silent house. Rhona didn't make the mistake of petting him; he'd scratched her arm and left a deep gouge on her first day back. Instead, she nipped upstairs for a shower.

The hot water revived her rain-chilled bones. She scrubbed the mud from her pores, then began her ritual of combing shampoo and conditioner through her long blonde hair. She wore it tied back so often it seemed pointless to make a thing out of keeping it hydrated, but she liked her hair. Gathering it together, she slipped it over to one side. The water gushed, clouding the room with steam. Rhona's awareness of her body brought images of Calum flooding back. *He's really getting to me. Why can't I stop thinking about him?* He was forbidden and that made it so much worse. 'Oh, god,' she moaned. Any other guy and they could have gone for a drink, a walk, whatever. But not him. They couldn't risk being seen together. It was bad enough trying to hide a dig in a remote corner of the island, never mind a public liaison. Especially if it led anywhere like the places Rhona was imagining. She finished off in the shower and wrapped herself in a huge towel.

The hair drying routine took even longer than the washing when she did it properly. Most days, she didn't bother; she tossed it into a ponytail and let the air do the job. But today she had time to pamper herself. The result was a surprisingly clean Rhona. She smiled at her reflection, golden locks bouncing round her shoulders, then peeked out the window. 'Seriously?'

The garden was basking in sunlight. All trace of rain had blown off to trouble another island. *Ridiculous Hebridean weather.* It never conformed to weather forecasts and frequently changed so randomly. Should she go back to the dig? When she'd finally cleaned up? No. The ground would be a quagmire and she couldn't face getting covered in it again.

Down in the garden, the summer house door opened; Judy ambled out and stretched. Whatever she was painting in there, Rhona still hadn't found out. But finished pictures of landscapes and seascapes adorned the walls. Her mum had a talent – one she didn't appreciate being interrupted. Exactly why Alister spent most of his days fishing, golfing or gardening.

Rhona picked up her phone and tapped it. Maybe Kirsten would be about? It was worth a try. She typed a message, then checked her emails. Taking on the work for Calum had happened at exactly the right time because the virtual research she'd been doing had dried up.

About an hour later, her phone buzzed.

KIRSTEN: Hi. I'll be back about five. Come down if you want and I'll show you the house. Fraser's on a late tour so I'd love the company!

Rhona checked the time. No great rush. But Uisken Bay where Kirsten and Fraser were building their new home was at the other end of the island and it took a long time to reach it on the twisty roads. Plus, Rhona had to persuade her mum to let her borrow the car.

'Where are you going?' Judy peered out from behind her easel.

'To Uisken to see Kirsten's new house.' Rhona kept her hands firmly planted in the back pockets of her jeans.

'That's quite a way. Are you sure you can do it?'

'Of course I can.'

'You haven't always been the most confident driver, you were the only one to fail your first test.'

Said like I was the only one in the world! But Judy meant the only one of her siblings. Summed up her life. She'd found that rare shell pottery on Crete but she didn't dare tell them. Alister would look up the report and find it published under the name of Annike Steib. How could she explain that? Arran was the only family member she'd told, half hoping he'd hunt Annike around the world until she told the truth but his reply had been flat. Maybe years of telling him to stop treating her like a child had paid off and he'd left her to do it herself.

'That was ages ago. I can drive fine now.' Though she hadn't for a while and the last time was a left-hand drive vehicle in Greece.

'Well, ok, darling. But please take care.'

'I will.'

She grabbed the keys and left before Judy could change her mind. If she was early, she could sit on the beach and relax or climb to the old burial site beyond. With the sun out it was a pleasant drive. She half expected a message from Calum telling her to get back to work. Maybe she just wished for one.

Uisken was one of the most picturesque beaches on the island. Tourists sometimes stumbled on it but today it was deserted and gloriously calm. Rhona crossed her legs on the sand and closed her eyes, listening to the waves, the gulls, and the flutter of long grass on the dunes in the gentle breeze. Calum might scoff at her for wanting to bond with nature but it was worth it. Tranquillity washed over her.

'Rhona.' A voice woke her from her reverie. How long had she sat in her silent meditation? From the small car park where she'd abandoned her mum's car, Kirsten waved. Rhona got to her feet and jogged over.

'Hey. I was totally zoned out.'

'I drove down to see if you were here,' Kirsten said. 'I thought you might be.'

'I think I drove past your new house.'

'You must have, it's the only road in and out.'

Rhona followed Kirsten back the way she'd come and pulled off the road into a newly cut opening behind a small croft. A field beneath a rocky hillock had been cleared and house foundations covered the ground like a 3D floor plan.

'Wow.' Rhona scanned around as Kirsten beamed at her building site. 'It's a great size and what a stunning location.'

'Isn't it? Fraser's gran, Agnes, lives in the croft there.'

'Oh, I remember.' Rhona smirked at Kirsten. Two summers ago, Rhona had been back on a visit with their other two besties, Ann-Marie and Cha – the group they called the Mullsketeers – but Kirsten had cried off one of their pub dates to deliver a missing phone to someone mysterious. Fraser. The enigmatic man who'd been living in a tent atop the hill behind his gran's house.

'Yeah, I bet you do.' Kirsten's cheeks glowed.

'Ironic you were the one who landed the guy who lived in a tent and goes about in a kilt, he sounds much more like my type.' Rhona cringed as she remembered eyeing him up in the pub before she'd realised Kirsten was after him – well, you couldn't blame a girl for looking. 'And if not me, then Cha. She likes a rugged man.' Their blue-haired Mullsketeer friend was easily the most rebellious of the gang. If Rhona had channelled some of her vibes on Crete, she'd have had no difficulty giving Annike a piece of her mind, or a fist in the face.

But it wasn't her style. She'd always shied away from conflict. Catriona and Mhairi, her older sisters, fought like cat and dog –

all the time. As teenagers their fights shook walls. Alister roared at them and Judy screamed for them to be quiet. Rhona, being much younger, just wanted them to stop. Tears flowed often as she pleaded with them to play dolls with her. She didn't need to hear what one had done to the other. Even now, they played off against each other and rarely got together through choice. Much as Rhona loved them, and individually enjoyed their company, she hated being pig in the middle at family gatherings.

She plonked her arm around Kirsten. 'This house is going to be gorgeous.'

'This is where we're staying at the moment.' Kirsten pointed at an old caravan. 'I'm not sure it's any better than the tent.'

'Can't you stay with his gran?'

'Fraser doesn't like to. He thinks he's imposing on her. And her croft is pretty small.'

'I guess, but so's that caravan.'

'We'll appreciate the house once it's up. How's your research going?'

Rhona glanced around. 'Listen, don't tell anyone and I'll let you into a secret.'

'I'm not sure I can keep secrets from Fraser.'

'Well, tell him if you like but warn him, I'll crack his nuts if he tells anyone.'

Kirsten laughed. 'Ok, that should do the trick.'

'So,' Rhona lowered her voice even though no one was around. 'I'm doing the dig at Kilnarkie.'

'No. Did Calum Matheson agree?'

'Yup. But no one else knows.' She pouted. 'Except Will Laird and his wife, but I think Calum has threatened him with something worse than nutcracking so hopefully he won't blab.'

'Your parents won't be happy.'

'What they don't know can't hurt. But I hate not telling them. I'm like a naughty teenager sneaking about, washing my dirty stuff in the sink before I put it in the machine, and keeping secrets.'

'It's probably for the best in the long run. Because you won't be there for too long, will you?'

'Another few weeks and that's about as long as I dare because Arran's coming back for a holiday, and if he finds out...' Rhona clenched her knuckles. 'He'll murder Calum. But it should be done by then, unless I unearth something special.'

'Do you think you will?'

'Probably not. It would be exciting if I did but Calum wouldn't be happy.'

'Why?'

'It's already taking too long and costing too much for his liking.'

'Oh dear. Is he awful to work for?'

Rhona huffed out a little laugh. 'He's not as grumpy as his reputation.'

Kirsten raised her eyebrows. 'We always thought you had a crush on him at school.'

'Don't be ridiculous.' There, she'd done it again, as she had back then, denied her interest because he wasn't cool enough. Who would have found the boy with the spotty face attractive? They'd have laughed her off the island. Rhona liked to fit in and not rock the boat.

Now, she couldn't admit it without going against her family. But this was an impartial friend. 'Maybe I did. A bit.'

Kirsten shook her head and laughed. 'I knew it. Wait until I tell Cha and Ann-Marie.'

'There's no need to spread it around like that.'

'Cha was more convinced than me. She spotted you doodling RL hearts CM on a jotter at school but you'd scribbled it out before she got a proper look. She had us watching constantly. All I ever noticed was that you went hysterical whenever he came anywhere near us. I remember one time he, Arran and Will were at the farm visiting Beth and you were itching to nosey at what they were doing, and when he walked in, you burst into a fit of giggles and couldn't talk for about an hour after.'

Rhona covered her face. 'I thought I was doing such a great job of hiding it but I was making it worse.' She sighed. 'I'm so glad those days are over.'

'I take it you don't still go into convulsions when you see him.'

'Not that kind, no.'

Kirsten put her hands on her hips. 'Explain that.'

Time to zip it? But if she couldn't confide in a friend, then who? The desperation to tell someone was burning a hole inside her. She could message Cha or the Mullsketeer group and have a less personal online discussion that might spare some of her blushes but Kirsten was here and available to listen.

'I still have a crush on him.'

'Seriously?'

'Yup. Every time I see him, I want to jump his hot body.'

'Oh my god. You are joking, aren't you?' Kirsten gaped, her expression torn between shock and pity.

Rhona shook her head. 'Nope. It's true. But nothing can happen.'

'Why?'

'Er, because he's Calum Matheson. The one whose family we don't speak to.'

'Wow. This is a proper little *Romeo and Juliet*.'

'Yeah, well, in a few weeks, we'll part ways and I'll forget all about him. I'm not that far gone that I'm going to drink a bottle of poison and die crying over a pair of his boxer shorts.' Though somewhere in a back cavity of her heart that was exactly what she wanted to do.

After skiving off on Thursday, Rhona made sure she was at the site bright and early on Friday. She left before either of her parents were up and stuck a note to the table saying she'd gone to see a friend. Partially true, though not one they'd approve of.

Calum had said he would come on Friday to check the week's work and Rhona's skin prickled. When would he arrive? She worked her way around the perimeter of the house's proposed footprint, marking off every area she considered part of the Iron Age dwelling and requiring further investigation. Realistically the remaining project could be done in a week. Eking it out to keep seeing Calum was silly.

Was she brave enough to suggest they kept in touch? Or more? Would he want to? He'd shown her enough to infer he liked her, but enough to defy his family? Could she defy hers?

'Nope.' She couldn't stand it if they disowned her. She slammed her pick into the ground. It was hopeless.

Time ticked on. The sun sat high in the sky with a ribbon of scattered clouds trailing across it. In the afternoon the wind picked up. Calum didn't show. At four thirty, she packed up, grabbed her notes and a pencil and started her write up. Why hadn't he come?

A message pinged and she grabbed her phone. Could it be him? Reception was so patchy, it could be something he'd sent hours ago and this was it just coming in.

CHA: I hear you have some gossip for me? Spill. What's happening? Kirsten says you're resurrecting something I should know about.

Rhona rolled her eyes. Not Calum then. Still, the chance to talk about him was a crumb in a day of slim pickings.

RHONA: I've resurrected an old crush. RL still hearts CM... Well, kind of! Lol. Not easy to crush on someone my family hate!

She'd barely set the phone down when a reply popped up.

CHA: Seriously! OMG.

CHA: He's the bastard who beat up Arran and left school because everyone hated him.

CHA: Isn't he some kind of Scrooge now?

CHA: What the hell are you doing crushing on him? Don't let him bully you into anything or I'll be back to sort him out!

'You and Arran both.' Whichever way she flipped it, Calum hadn't made himself popular. He definitely had a dodgy past but... it didn't fit with who he was now.

A car engine rumbled, and she glanced up. Calum's dark grey 4X4. He jumped out and craned his neck over the roof. When he spotted her, he waved, slammed the door and jogged up the hill to the trench.

Her feet dangled over the edge as she watched him; her pulse drummed in her ears. He was so damn hot in that black t-shirt and those tight jeans. Warnings danced around her head. Treat him like an employer, ignore all sensations, however pleasant, however persistent. But it was hard... too hard.

'Are you in a rush to get home?' he called from a distance.

'Not especially, why?'

'Good. Wait there. I've got something for you.' He turned back to his car.

What was he up to? His boot slammed and he appeared again carrying an old-fashioned picnic basket. He made his way around beside her and set it on the ground. His cushion was rolled up on top of it. Rhona's lips twitched as he unfurled it and sat beside her. 'Dinner?' He opened the basket.

'Oh my goodness. This is a bit of a posh picnic.'

'Uh-huh. This is to prove that I can do outdoors too.'

She laughed and held his blue-green irises in hers, gazing at the flecks of light twinkling in them. Her heartrate multiplied. So much for keeping things professional. She was ready to fall on his lips. Nerve ends tingled, urging her closer. He'd done this for her. Maybe to prove a point but he'd still done it. 'You can, Mr Matheson. In your own special way.'

'Let's eat it then, Miss Lamond, and you can summarise the week for me... In *your* own special way.' He flicked her a pointed look and raised an eyebrow. 'Sorry, I'm so late. I meant to get here ages ago but I got held up at the flats. I thought you might have gone.'

'I was waiting for you.'

His brow furrowed. 'Were you?'

'You said you'd come.'

'I did. But you didn't have to hang about. You could have emailed the summary to me.'

'I didn't mind waiting.'

He picked up a roll and opened a container of salad. His eyelids flickered like he was processing too many thoughts at once.

Rhona was famished; she'd been so engrossed in her work she'd forgotten to eat lunch. So much delicious food was crammed into the basket. Where to start?

After gorging on sourdough rolls and cheese, she lolled back propping herself up on her arms, palms on the grass, and threw back her head. When she slid her focus to Calum, he swallowed and moved his focus from her chest to her face. 'So, shall I give it to you?' she asked.

'Pardon?' He choked on a mouthful of food.

'My summary.' She quirked her eyebrow, holding back a giggle.

'Sure.' He cleared his throat.

'So...' She lifted her notes and read out the main points. 'Another week should do it.'

'That's all?' He threw the empty containers back into the basket.

'It'll take me a while to write the report but the groundwork should be done by next Friday. Unless there's torrential rain for a week.'

'Let's not count it out. It won't be the first time.'

'But you don't have to pay me if I'm not on site.' She stretched over the picnic basket and pressed her fingers on his arm to reassure him.

He glanced at her hand, then back to her face. 'I know.'

'I'll miss it here.'

Calum shut the picnic basket lid and shoved it behind him. Rhona took it as an invitation and shuffled up beside him.

'This has been ok, hasn't it?' She peered up at him, swinging her legs.

'What has?'

'A Matheson and a Lamond working together.'

'It's been an eye-opener.'

Rhona checked her cleavage in case she'd dropped a grape or something onto it and he was actually alluding to that. Everything looked normal. She swallowed, then gently nudged her head against his shoulder. 'I haven't uncovered treasure but this place has opened a whole new world for me.'

'I'm glad.' His body stiffened but he didn't move away.

Rhona closed her eyes, still leaning her ear on him. 'Thanks for trusting me and letting me do it.'

'I would say anytime but I'm not sure I want a repeat of this.'

She lifted her head to withdraw, but his arm swept around her before she could move. He cupped her shoulder. Wow. His palm was so warm. Being held like this, however light his touch was, gave her an overpowering sense of being special, important and wanted.

'I don't mean you. I mean, I don't want to have any more archaeological digs on my land. From a purely miserly point of view.'

With a sigh, she leaned on him again. Slowly, she crept her fingertips to his thigh and gently squeezed it. Forward maybe, but it was visceral. She wanted to touch him. He twitched and put his own hand over hers.

'You're a very nice person,' he said. 'For a Lamond.'

'Cheeky, Mr Matheson.' Their gazes met. She held eye contact for as long as she dared. The sparkometer burst into overdrive. *Is he going to kiss me? Am I going to kiss him?* Something was going to happen. Wasn't it? The charge in the air was unmistakable. She kept staring until he uncurled her fingers from his thigh. Slowly, he turned over her hand, raised it to his lips and gently kissed the inside of her wrist.

Her heart stopped. She closed her eyes. That had to be the most sensual thing anyone had ever done to her. *Take me wherever you want to...*

'Right.' Calum gently released her. 'We should get moving.'

'We should... Should we?' She blinked. That was it?

'Uh-huh.' He jumped to his feet and lifted the picnic basket. 'Do you want a lift down the road?'

'Um, no thank you. I'd like to walk.'

'Ok. Well, you have a great weekend and I'll see you on Monday.'

'See you.' She raised her hand weakly. Her wrist ached for more of his kisses. But his car door slammed, the engine rumbled and he was gone. *Just like that. Wow, ok.* After the buzz, the build-up, the feelings she was sure they shared, he was ok with driving off alone.

She wrapped her arms around herself and sat for a long time staring at the sky. Maybe he was the smart one but where did that leave her and her aching heart?

Chapter Twelve

Calum

Calum had crossed lines before. In business, he had to cross lines to get results. He didn't break the law; he just knew how to make things work in his favour. With Arran he'd broken the karate code and attacked him rather than using the moves for self-defence. Now he'd stepped over a whacking-big line with Rhona.

'I kissed her, for Christ's sake,' he muttered to himself. If he hadn't done it on her wrist, he'd have planted one on her lips. That would have been worse. Wouldn't it? Maybe not. Something about kissing her there had been so intimate and erotic. And her reaction. She'd tripped out. Having that power over her from one little kiss was terrifying. But energising. He could give her so much more if she wanted it. 'Just stop!' This wasn't what he was supposed to be doing. He was digging a hole bigger than the trench.

Between Rhona, the dig, and his tenants, he'd clean forgotten about the annual Midsummer fair that Sunday. It wasn't something he particularly cared about but he liked to show face at events, partly to let people know he wasn't intimidated by the Lamonds. His parents were the same. The gossips had a field day if Ron and Alister were spotted in the beer tent at the same time.

Ron appeared tough with his burly frame and his tattoos but he was the world's biggest softy at heart. He cried at the slightest thing on TV and befriended the friendless. He was famous for adopting all and sundry and chatting to everyone wherever he went – as long as it wasn't a Lamond.

To go or not to go? Rhona might be there. It was in Dervaig, close to where she lived. Message her and ask? No. He didn't want his text to be misconstrued as anything other than a simple question. She might think he was asking her on a date or because he was desperate to see her again. Which he was. But a move like that? Too blunt. How rich coming from the twat who'd kissed her on the wrist when he should be keeping a professional distance. But the buzz that thrummed between them every time they were close was impossible to ignore.

Arriving late was the best plan – not easy as the fair went on until midnight – but it would mean only a short time there. A bright blue sky heralded a clear evening. Everything was set up outside, including an area for dancing. Good, good. Because the indoor space wasn't big enough to hide in. Calum sat in the car, listening to the ceilidh music from the field and tapping the wheel. He could do this. Rhona might not even be there. If she was, he'd play it cool. He focused on his breathing for several minutes, then got out and strode towards the field in the evening sunshine.

He visualised Rhona dressed in a sheer white gown, hugging her curves, her long blonde hair flowing around her shoulders and down her back, a circlet of flowers in her hair as she worshipped the sun gods on the longest day of the year. He rolled his neck, alleviating the remaining tension and searching for a familiar face.

'Hello, son.' A thick hand clapped him on the back. 'Long time, no see.'

'Hi, Dad. What do you mean? I saw you the other day.'

'Aye, aye,' Ron said. 'Because I happened to be passing your office.'

'I've been busy, haven't I?'

'No doubt, no doubt.'

'Where's Mum?'

'God knows. Chatting to someone for a change.'

Calum scanned the field, partly looking for his mum but mostly seeking Rhona.

'What's going on at the Gruline house?' Ron said.

'What do you mean?' Heavy doom filled Calum's chest at the mention of the place.

'I met the tenants and they said there were lots of problems but they can never get hold of you.'

'Seriously?' Calum pinched the bridge of his nose. 'That is utter rubbish. I'm at that bloody house every week about something or other.'

'I told them you were busy.'

'I've been at Kilnarkie quite a bit. There was an archaeological condition attached to my planning permission, so I've been sorting that out.'

'That doesn't sound too good. How will you get around that?'

'I have a contractor.' He didn't look at his dad. If he did, he was sure he would somehow betray himself and Ron would know a Lamond was involved. From across the field, his mum's burgundy hair bobbed into view. She waved before shimmying over in her bright pink outfit.

'Calum, darling, you look as gorgeous as ever, my lovely, lovely boy.' She slapped her palms on either side of his face and pulled him down for a kiss. For the first time in a long while, Calum slid his arms around her back and hugged her.

'Hey, Mum.'

'Oh, my darling. Is everything ok?'

'Uh-huh.'

'He's having to deal with *archaeological conditions*.' Ron air quoted.

'What the hell is that? You're not ill, are you?'

'No.' Calum explained, carefully skirting around mentioning who was doing the work, and deliberately making it sound like nothing had happened yet.

'I bet those Lamonds reported you again.' Anne screwed up her nose. 'They've done shit like that in the past.'

'Bloody awful people the lot of them,' Ron muttered.

'I don't think they did.' Calum weighed the thought in his mind. 'An objection wouldn't come up as an archaeological condition.' He frowned. Maybe it would. Maybe it had. His sceptical brain took over for a few moments. Had they interfered? If so, where did that leave him?

'I saw them at the baking stall.' Anne rolled her eyes. 'One of their daughters is back living with them, the youngest one. They're fawning over her like she's a princess. She must be in her late twenties by now, but they're acting like she's about eighteen.'

'I heard she was back,' Ron said. 'Wonder what she's doing here.'

'Not sure.' Anne rippled her fingertips together. 'I can easily find out what business she went into.'

Calum cleared his throat, his mind reeling. 'There's Will. Have you met baby Angus yet?'

At the edge of the field, Will and Morven ambled around the stalls, Angus strapped to Morven's front, his little head resting forward, clearly sleeping. The perfect distraction.

'Aw, yes. He's such a cutie,' Anne said. Will and Morven approached. Will waved enthusiastically. 'He reminds me of you. Never slept at home but the minute we went out somewhere you'd go out like a light. Everyone said what a great baby you must be sleeping like that. But the minute we got home, ping! Your eyes would open and that was it.'

Calum held out his palms. 'Sorry.'

'Hello, hello,' Will said. 'I didn't know you were coming, Calum.'

'Thought I'd drop in for a minute or two.'

'We're heading home. Hopefully our little guy will stay sleeping for a bit.'

Anne peered round at the sleeping baby and gently stroked his forehead with a scarlet-tipped finger. 'He's a wee angel but if he's anything like Calum he'll wake up the minute you get in the door.'

Calum facepalmed and Will chortled. 'That might be the case, but we'll see. We need a catch up soon. I'm dying to hear the news from Kilnarkie.' He winked.

'Nothing to tell.' Calum fixed him with a pointed glare. 'Everything's exactly as it should be.'

'That's something.' Will grinned.

Angus gave a little cry. Morven stroked his back and swayed him. 'We should be off and try and get him into bed.'

'Good luck and see you soon.' Calum waved them off. 'I might mingle for a bit.'

'Ok, son,' Ron clapped his back.

Throwing his hands into his pockets, Calum strolled around the field, nodding to some familiar faces. Would his mum follow through on nosing into what Rhona did these days? She knew so many people; someone was sure to know Rhona had gone into archaeology. Now he'd mentioned the archaeological condition, it wouldn't be a big leap to make to place her at the dig. The island wasn't exactly crawling with archaeologists. At least his parents would never suspect him of teaming up with a Lamond. How unlikely was it? Yet, he'd let it happen. The intense hatred he harboured for that family had mutated into something equally powerful with Rhona but about as far from hate as he could get.

Uh-oh. Blair and Rebekah were heading his way. This time last year, he might have been jealous at the sight of them arm in arm and looking so loved-up. But now? He flexed his fingers. Nothing. His heart was wholly consumed by the woman with the evil surname.

'Hello.' He edged towards them.

'Hi, Calum.' Rebekah greeted him with a pat on the shoulder.

'All right?' Blair said.

'Yeah, all good, thanks.'

'How's the work at Kilnarkie?' Rebekah asked. 'Are you any further forward?'

'Yes and no,' Calum said. 'It doesn't look like it'll be suitable for the housing project. I've been working with an archaeologist and she's already made discoveries on the current plot. If I reapply to build more houses, there'll be further conditions and who knows what might turn up. It's too costly and time-consuming.'

'It sounds it,' Rebekah said. 'But I'm sure we'll find another site.'

'Yes, things will come up and...' He trailed off. His eyes detoured. Rhona was crossing the field. Her floaty pink dress was even better than the one he'd imagined. The neckline scooped low and was tied with a string bow. The skirt cascaded over her hips and swished around her knees as she strolled along chatting to friends. Her long hair fell around her shoulders and, though she didn't have the crown of flowers, two clips held it back from her forehead. Her rosy cheeks glowed. A picture of perfection. Calum's mouth opened but no words came out. She zeroed in on him and the corners of her peachy lips quirked up. Pushing a strand of hair behind her ear, she fluttered her lashes. Calum blinked back at Rebekah and Blair. Did they know about the issues with the Lamonds? Blair was an islander, so it was likely.

'And what?' Blair cocked his head.

'Hmm?' Calum rubbed his chin. 'I, erm. Can you excuse me a minute? I remembered something I need to do.'

Leave. That was what he had to do. Find his parents, say goodbye and go. Seeing Rhona wafting about like a princess was tormenting. And really that was the reason he was here. He wanted to see her. But seeing her and being with her were two different things. The first was just creepy and stalkerish.

Head bowed, he strode around the edge of the field, close to the verge which led down a hill towards the sea.

'Calum.'

He recognised her voice before he turned.

'Am I allowed to talk to you?' Rhona asked.

'About what?'

'I mean in general, or will people put two and two together and make fifty-six?'

'Exactly that.' Fire licked his insides. 'So, no. You shouldn't talk to me here. My parents are already getting curious about the dig and you being back. I don't want them making any connection between us or doing anything that might jeopardise my family. We can talk on Monday. At the dig.'

She tilted her head and her blue eyes dulled. 'Ok. It's such a shame it has to be like this.'

Calum shoved his hands in his pockets, shifted his feet and glanced down. A persistent thud in his chest urged him to look back. He mustn't. Looking was like holding the key to the forbidden door. 'Let's not start anything we'll end up regretting.' A warning to himself as much as her. A fine line was all that remained between them. Crossing it would be easy and maybe the only way to satisfy his cravings. But oh so risky.

'Ok. Well, see you at the dig then.'

'Yeah. See you.' Her dress swished as she trotted away.

If she could be anyone else. Anyone at all. Just not a Lamond.

Chapter Thirteen

Rhona

The spark had hit. The one Rhona had been waiting for forever. Every guy she'd ever dated had undergone her sparkometer test and most of them had barely registered. Until Calum. He'd spiked the dial the day she'd seen him marching towards her across his land and since then it had revved irrevocably upward. When he'd kissed her wrist on Friday the readings had been off the scale. Then he'd left. His coldness at the fair spoke volumes. And he was right, they shouldn't do anything in the heat of the moment that could lead to regrets later on.

But would a few minutes of stolen pleasure be so bad? One day in the near future she'd be off on a job somewhere and would have to leave him behind anyway. Would settling for a clandestine fling satisfy her in the short term? Did Calum do things like that? Unlikely. He seemed to want to return to a professional relationship.

'Why can't I feel the same?' Rhona asked Nelson as he flexed his claws into her duvet. He'd taken to lying on her bed while she worked on her laptop at the dressing table – probably so he could keep his beady eye on her. 'I shouldn't be hoping for anything else. I need to be professional.' Easier said than done. The sparkometer urged her to seek more. 'It's worse than a crush. For all I know it could still be the nonsense from school.' Maybe it was a latent rebellion to her family's mollycoddling over the years. Good little Rhona, the peacekeeper, had grown horns.

Must get over this now. She stayed away from the dig that morning to test out some software. Keying in as much data as she could, she came up with a basic site reconstruction. As the software was only for her use while she was ad hoc working for the research company, she wouldn't be able to keep the work, but it fascinated her. This was exactly what she wanted to do but she couldn't afford the outlay if she wanted to do this independently.

'Calum would like to see this,' she informed Nelson, jumping to her feet and grabbing her phone from the windowsill. Her fingers hovered over the screen. This was purely professional, right? She wanted to show him the reconstruction. Nothing else. The lightness in her head said otherwise. But if she didn't show him this, she'd regret it. 'It's work, just work.' She keyed in his number.

He answered on the second ring, taking her by surprise. Sometimes he was impossible to get hold of. Had he been waiting for her to call? 'Hi. What's up? Have you discovered treasure?'

'No.' She grinned at the mix of cheer and panic in his voice. 'I've been trying out some software I have on loan and I've made a reconstruction of the dig. I'd love you to see it. Can you come over? Or are you mega busy as usual?'

'I am, yes. Come over where? Are you at Kilnarkie?'

'No, I'm—'

'You don't mean your parents' house, do you? I can't come there.'

'It's ok, they're out. Dad's gone fishing, he'll be away all day and Mum's out for lunch with friends. I don't expect her back for ages.'

'Hmm.'

Rhona could almost hear his brain ticking over the idea. Maybe inviting him to the house wasn't just unprofessional but downright crazy.

'Ok, I'll come over, but I'm at my office so it'll take me half an hour.'

He would? 'Great!' Rhona did a jig on the spot as she ended the call. Nelson looked her up and down, then licked his paw, almost tutting. 'It's still work, I swear.'

So much for keeping away from him. But this was business. She itched to pick stuff up and tidy it away, but Judy kept the house so spotless, there was nothing to do. She paced, leapt to the windows for any sign of anything, and chewed on a cuticle. This might go horribly wrong.

A knock on the door. What? No cars had pulled up. She checked out the window. Nothing indicated anyone was there. She bounded downstairs to open the door. Through the frosted glass, she could tell it was Calum from his broad-shouldered outline before she pulled the handle.

'Hi.' She tugged open the door. 'Where's your car?'

'I left it on the verge round the corner in case your parents come back.' He stroked his hand over his neatly trimmed dark hair, disturbing the air and generating a cloud of expensive body spray that tickled her senses.

She stepped aside to let him in, admiring another of his trademark outfits: the tight dark skinny jeans and Converse-style boots, today paired with a grey t-shirt that clung to hidden ridges of muscle, and a navy blazer. 'They won't be back for hours.'

'Yeah? It'd be just my luck.' Calum scanned around. 'I haven't been here for years. What is it you want me to see?'

'Come up to my bedroom.' Rhona tucked her hair behind her ear, cringingly aware of how that had sounded. The whole situation could be misconstrued as a setup. Was it? Had her subconscious tricked her?

'Seriously?' Calum arched an eyebrow, the tiniest smile playing on his lips. 'Is this legit?'

'Why wouldn't it be?' Rhona attempted to sound innocent but it came out too fast and too defensive.

'No idea.' Calum glanced at the stairs. 'Up we go then.'

Heat fired in her cheeks as she climbed the stairs and opened her bedroom door.

'Are you sure I'm allowed in here?' Calum's tone was even more sceptical. 'The last time I was in this house, a giggling teenager lived in this room and I wouldn't have dared look in the door.'

'Yeah. Thankfully she's grown up.' Rhona crossed the room to her dressing table where she'd set up her laptop. *Why didn't I move the bloody thing downstairs?* The subconscious was working overtime today. 'You can sit on the bed. Just watch Nelson. He scratches and bites.'

Calum and the cat glared at each other for a few seconds. 'I'll stand.'

'Ok.' Rhona sat on her stool and pulled up the site reconstruction. 'This is what I wanted to show you. Once I get it on the screen, you can take this seat and have a look.' She waited for it to load, then stood.

Calum took her place, frowning at the screen. Rhona hovered behind him, tapping her toes inside her fluffy slippers, wishing he would say something. He navigated around, his eyes narrowing, but didn't speak. Was it that bad? Was he offended? Had she crossed some boundary? After all, this wasn't in her contract, it was something she'd done because she wanted to.

Had she got this all wrong? Was this another epic fail? If he would just speak. Or stand up, walk out and say she was fired... She'd deal with it.

'What are you thinking?' She couldn't hold it in any longer.

Calum shook his head. 'This is unbelievable.'

'Good unbelievable or bad unbelievable?'

'Good. Amazing.'

Rhona covered her mouth as her muscles relaxed. He didn't hate it. And better, he liked it. She lifted her chin and let out a little laugh. 'I thought you were annoyed that I'd done it instead of going to the dig.'

'Is this the kind of thing you usually do on a dig?'

'No.' Rhona flopped onto the edge of the bed. 'I've never been involved in this kind of thing. I've always wanted to but it's above my paygrade usually. The software isn't mine. It belongs to the company I'm doing the research work for, so I won't be able to keep any of this.'

'Can't we pay to keep it? I'd hate it going to waste. It's such an amazing representation. At the dig I just see mud and holes dug in the ground. But this makes sense of it. I'd love to show it to people.'

Rhona smiled, feeling taller, more confident, more important. 'You can buy the completed reconstruction and use it wherever you want. But I wouldn't be able to add anything to it after that.'

'Find out how much. I really want it. This explains it so well to idiots like me who can't visualise it.'

'You're hardly an idiot.'

'You're so talented, you know?' Calum swivelled on the stool to face her. Their eyes met and resumed their silent bonding. 'You're wasted in what you do. Not entirely, you're good at that too, but this…' He gestured back to the screen. 'Is just wow.'

Rhona glanced at her feet and sucked in her lips. 'It was mostly the software.'

'No, Rhona. It was mostly you. You can work the software and get it to look like a dig that only you and I have seen. That's you, not the computer.'

She tilted her head. 'Thanks.'

Calum slapped his thighs and got to his feet. 'So, find out about the cost and let me know.' He made his way to the door and Rhona followed. At the bottom of the stairs, he peeked into the open-plan living area and out towards the garden. 'It's changed so much. That summer house looks amazing. It's the kind of thing I want for my office when I upgrade the container.'

'That's my mum's studio. No one's allowed in. She's very precious about it.'

'Is she? So, I better not go snooping around then. Imagine me not only getting caught here but getting caught in her private studio.'

'It's locked and she probably has the key, so you couldn't get in anyway. I could show you in the window if you want.'

'Not a great plan.'

'You only live once.'

'I thought you'd reincarnated several times through your Iron Age people?'

'Haha. Come on.' Rhona giggled and grabbed her trainers from the front porch.

'I have a bad feeling about this and I'm not someone who's prone to that kind of thing.'

She led the way into the garden. 'Out of luck.' The blinds were drawn.

'What does she do in there that it's so top secret?'

'She paints, but she doesn't like anyone seeing what she's done until she's finished.'

'A real perfectionist.'

'Totally and utterly.'

Calum slung his hands in his back pockets and surveyed the garden. 'It's a lovely spot. And you've still got the tree house. I always wanted a tree house, but our garden wasn't suitable. No trees.'

'Do you want to have a look?'

'I won't fit in it.'

'You will. Come and see. The view's amazing. I cleaned it out when I came home. I like going up there and watching the sea.' Rhona crossed the garden and climbed the slightly dodgy ladder. She hauled herself in and sat on the edge, peeking down. Calum was still at the bottom, frowning and squinting around.

'Come on.' She tapped her foot on the step.

'This is not wise.'

'It's fine, honestly.'

He put his foot on the bottom rung. It creaked. 'I'm not sure this'll hold my weight.'

'Seriously? You're a skinny rake. I probably weigh more than you.'

'I don't think so, somehow. You're titchy.'

'If only. I'm average height and... curvy.'

'Nothing wrong with that. Looks pretty good to me.'

Heat scorched her cheeks. He really thought that?

He tested the step again, then made his way up. 'Well, shift over. Are you sure there's room in there for both of us?'

'Kind of.'

'And it won't fall?'

'It's fairly stable. I didn't realise you were so nervous.'

'I'm not normally. But how do I know this hasn't been booby-trapped against Mathesons?'

Rhona shuffled into the corner with a grin as Calum hoisted himself in through the hatch. A patch of dust streaked his navy blazer and he scraped more from his jeans. 'I see you cleaned this brilliantly.'

'I forgot about your clean fetish.'

'It is not a fetish. There's nothing wrong with liking to be clean.'

Rhona suppressed a giggle. 'Look at the view and see if it was worth it.'

Calum climbed onto his knees. 'I should have brought my cushion.' He leaned on the ledge and peered out. 'It is a good view though. Shame it's a bit cloudy today. I guess I take the views here for granted.' He crawled around the hatch and parked next to Rhona. 'I should go. I have lots still to do. Thanks for helping me release my inner crazy again.' He swung his legs over the edge.

'What do you mean?'

'Whenever I'm with you I end up doing something mad.'

'Do you mean dirty?'

'I'm not sure I do.' He threw her a look over his shoulder and she covered her face.

'Oh my god, that sounded so dodgy.'

'That's your MO though, isn't it?' He gave a dry laugh and she peeked through her fingers. When he smiled, he was irresistible. His sea-green eyes sparkled. The sun poked through the clouds sending dappled shadows through the window.

'I once caught Arran snogging his girlfriend up here.' Rhona smirked.

'Don't tell me – Hannah McDonald.'

'How did you know that?'

'Because she was the girl I liked, so... Er, never mind.'

'Well... I have a confession too.'

'Oh, Jesus, what? You've found some precious treasure at the dig?' He half turned so he was facing her, his legs still hanging over the edge.

'No, nothing like that.' Her cheeks burned. 'I used to have a crush on you at school.'

He stared at her and his dark eyebrows met in the middle. 'On me? I don't think so.'

'Definitely on you.'

'Yeah, right. The acne-faced teen who reduced you to fits of giggles. I'm not that green.'

'That's the point. The giggles were to cover it up. I couldn't exactly shout it from the rooftops. You're four years older than me and at school that's a big gap.'

A muscle in his jaw twitched. 'Nothing to do with the fact I looked like I had permanent chickenpox and people called me the leper?'

'Not really. Maybe I was a bit embarrassed to like you.'

'I bet.'

'But...' She slipped her hand over his where it was resting on the dusty wooden edge. 'I always wanted to find out about the boy inside.'

'Did you?'

'Yup. I went to Arran's football club every week, hoping you'd be there.'

'I never liked football. I avoided hanging out after school because it was bad enough having people rip the piss out of me during the day. My dad took me to karate at the weekends.'

'I didn't know that.'

'I still do it.'

'Do you?'

'Uh-huh.' He straightened and his chin jutted forward. 'I'm a black belt now.'

'Wowsers. You must be brilliant.'

'I'm out of training, which is frustrating because I've got a competition coming up.'

'Wow, I'd like to see that.'

'Why?'

'Because my thirteen-year-old self still lives in me and quite fancies the idea of you hot and sweaty.'

'Keep talking like that and you'll get your wish.' He tugged at his neckline. Rhona shuffled forward and stared at him until he looked back.

She held his gaze. 'Calum... I really... I...' She beckoned him closer.

'What?'

She shuffled closer, unable to pull her focus from him. Her heart thundered in her ears.

'What are you doing?' His voice was less than a whisper.

'Can I give you a kiss? A teeny tiny one?' She mirrored his hushed tone.

His eyes fixed on her and lit up. He licked his lips very slightly. Rhona's pulse rate skyrocketed.

'Yes. I've wanted to ever since—' He leaned forward and sealed his lips over hers. The pointer on the sparkometer spun right off and snapped. She slid her fingers around his jaw and he peppered her with slow yet powerful kisses.

'Me too.'

They melted together. Rhona's stomach burned with desperation and she opened her mouth, her tongue found his and fireworks erupted deep inside.

If they could let go of the Matheson versus Lamond angst, she could do this every day. Calum broke away just as she was getting into it. He hoisted his legs inside so they were side by side, facing each other. 'That was...' He swallowed, threading his fingertips into the hair above her ear.

'What?'

'Insane.' He withdrew his fingers and trailed them over her cheek.

Rhona pulled herself onto her knees and looked down on him, her chest thrust forward. He raised his eyes to her and it was all the invitation she needed. She clutched his face again and kissed him. His body stiffened. Would he pull away? *Please no.* Palpitations attacked her. Then he relaxed and kissed her back. Their tongues met again, and an electric shock struck her deep. Calum's hands slipped around her waist, moving restlessly. She owned his mouth, moaning as she let herself go. This was so hot; much better than anything she'd imagined at thirteen. At twenty-eight, it brought a rush of pleasure.

A car door thumped in the distance and Calum pulled back. 'What the hell are we doing?'

'I don't know, but my god it's good.'

She resumed the kiss but Calum pulled away almost immediately, Rhona still nibbling on his lower lip. Her ears pricked. A sound like a door opening and closing reached their ears. Rhona let him go and, still on her knees, shuffled to the window and peeked out.

'Shit. My mum's back.'

Judy sauntered across the lawn towards her studio.

'How the hell can I get out of here?' Calum said.

'I'll go and talk to her.' Rhona straightened her t-shirt. 'You can climb down and jump the fence onto the road.'

'Jesus.' He threw his head back and leaned on the wall. 'Without her seeing me?'

'I'll keep her talking.' Rhona slumped her bottom onto her heels. 'But I need to get out first. I'll have to climb over you.'

'Any excuse.'

She smirked and rolled her lips together. *You're not wrong.* Pushing one knee over, she straddled him. Their eyes met and she had to have him. He got there first. His arms shot around her, gliding his long fingers over her curves, still maintaining eye contact.

'Let me take you away.' His lips were so close.

'What do you mean?'

'On my boat. Come with me. Just you and me, we can get away from everyone.'

'Yes. Oh god, yes. When?' She wiggled her hips, searching for a hotspot.

He drew in a rapid breath. 'This weekend.'

'Ok.' She held her forehead against his and inhaled slowly. She didn't remember ever wanting anyone this much.

Bending her neck, she sank onto his lips, grinding her hips at the same time. The rush of fire through her tummy made her gasp. She drowned him with kisses, thrusting her tongue into his welcoming mouth. He groaned and slid his hands around the curves of her bottom.

'Rhona.' His voice was a whispered growl. 'Please, get off me and get out. We can't go on like this. Not here, not now. Save it.'

She swallowed and composed herself. 'You're so annoyingly right.' As she steadied her breathing, her chest heaved up and down. Calum squeezed his eyes shut and turned away as though forcing himself not to look. 'Right, I'm going.' She swung her leg over and slid out the hatch, finding the ladder with her foot. 'Get ready to run.'

'Run? I can hardly move, never mind run.'

Rhona gave him a quick wink and descended, hoping her mum hadn't broken the habit of a lifetime and was in her studio with the blind drawn, noticing nothing except her painting.

Chapter Fourteen

Calum

Calum slumped against the wall in the tree house. *What the hell just happened?* Years ago, Arran had snogged Hannah McDonald in here. The same girl he'd later called a fat slut, fuelling the rage in Calum that had eventually sent him over the edge. And now Calum had kissed Arran's sister. The irony. But, Christ, what a kiss. Rhona was all excitement and enthusiasm. No finesse, just Rhona. Rhona. God, he wanted her. Now, he needed to calm down but he couldn't hang about.

With a groan, he dragged himself to the window. Rhona dallied at the studio door, hands in the back pockets of her shorts, her chest thrust out. *Christ.* Why did she do that? It made her too delicious. Her pink t-shirt clung to each curve, accentuating her perfect breast shape, her slender waist and generous hips. Flesh memories of where those parts had touched scorched him from the inside out. Kissing and cuddling weren't his thing so why was that all he wanted to do?

It could wait until Saturday. He had no choice. Once they were on the boat, they could go anywhere; far from prying eyes and gossiping tongues.

From the lawn, Rhona glanced sideways, slipped her fingers up her arm and rested her thumb up on the bare skin beneath the sleeve of her t-shirt. The cue to move. Slipping his legs over the edge, he felt around with his foot. Each step creaked as he made his way down. He screwed up his face but couldn't bear to look round. What if he'd been spotted? His feet hit the ground and he glimpsed Rhona still at the summer house door. Without wasting another second, he legged it across the garden, vaulted the wall and jogged along the road, round the bend to where he'd left the car.

His jacket and jeans were covered in dust. Unpleasant reminders of an otherwise very pleasant encounter. Pleasant but not sensible. He pulled out his phone to message her and a woozy sensation came over him. He opened the car door and flopped into his seat. His head whirred. Whichever way he swung it he'd asked Rhona out. In the heat of the moment, yes, but there was no getting around it. He was going on a date with the sister of his nemesis.

His fingers moved over the message but his mind was elsewhere. How would they fill the day? His dates followed a set pattern: dinner somewhere smart, a second dinner somewhere else, followed by a third. If they were still ok after that, he might invite them back. They rarely lasted after that. He didn't do fifth dates.

CALUM: Back in the car. That was an interesting morning. Remember to find out the cost of keeping the reconstruction. See you at the dig later in the week.

He didn't sign it with a kiss. It would be a lie to say he didn't want more, but a little *X* in a message wouldn't satisfy anything.

When he passed the house, Rhona was still at the summer house door, checking her phone. His lit up with two sharp beeps.

Back at his office, he checked the message.

RHONA: An interesting morning?!?! Hot more like! My mum saw nothing and doesn't suspect a thing. I wish we didn't have to sneak about, but I'm really excited about the boat trip. You're fulfilling one of my fantasies... Maybe more *wink emoji* Roll on the weekend! XXXXXXX

Calum shook his head. So much for not bothering with any more kisses. But that was Rhona. Other people might have been satisfied with a gentle kiss, but Rhona wanted six or seven, all intense, all passionate, an affection overload. He rubbed his hand over his forehead. Come Saturday, he needed to be prepared for whatever she threw at him. His mind and his heart raced in tandem. A thrill ricocheted through him.

With nervous tension building in his system, he prioritised his week, altering his diary to ensure he was anywhere but at the dig. What if they got caught together on Friday afternoon and had to call everything off? He didn't want anything to ruin this.

He messaged Rhona, apologising that he had to sort out his Gruline property. Not a lie. Those tenants were constantly moaning.

Rhona's reply told him she was almost finished. His heart sank. *What happens then?* Could they keep on seeing each other or would she fade away? Come Saturday, he would get a better sense for what was going on. Thinking beyond that filled him with fluff or messy visions of his parents' faces and Rhona's family. A shot at something bigger would slash into a lot of other relationships. Was it worth it? Life had no guarantees. He couldn't cut off his family for a fling. What was to stop Rhona leaving in a few weeks, abandoning him with no one and nothing? He couldn't risk it. 'What we're doing is transient,' he told his laptop. Rhona would pass and fade like the others.

'Your boat's called the Dawn Treader?' Rhona's gaze skimmed over the gleaming white yacht. Calum had given her a lift from the end of her garden into Tobermory where his boat was moored at the marina. At this time in the morning only a handful of people were about. Still, the crew on the fishing boats might recognise him or Rhona, so he was keen for her to get on board quickly.

'What's wrong with that? Don't you like C.S. Lewis?'

'I do but I didn't have you down as a fan.'

'There's lots you don't know about me, Miss Lamond.'

She beamed and eyed him over. 'I'd like to find out, Mr Matheson.'

'Let's stop talking.' He pressed his finger to his lips. 'You never know who might be listening. Now, jump aboard and I'll get her ready.'

Dressed in her purple waterproof and jeans, Rhona looked ready for a dig. She slung off her backpack and laid it on a bench. 'This boat is stunning.'

'What's in the backpack?' Calum raised an eyebrow. 'I've already stocked up on food.'

'Mostly clothes.'

'Clothes? How long are you planning on being away?'

She giggled. 'Just today. But the last time I went on a boat trip in Scotland, I dressed for a cold day and ended up roasting. The time before was the opposite. So, this time I'm prepared for whatever the weather throws at us.'

'Sounds sensible.'

'The forecast said sun, rain and possible high winds.'

'I noticed that.' Calum lifted the final tarp. 'Let's get going. It's nice just now.' He climbed into the cabin and Rhona followed.

'Calum.' She grabbed his wrist and pulled him back.

'Yes?'

Before he could get another word out, she threw her arms around his neck. 'I'm so happy we're doing this.'

He gripped her waist; his fingertips twitched with the urge glide over her – *save it*. 'Me too.' He gazed into her dreamy blue eyes. Her curves pitched into all the right places. Like a magnet was pulling him, he dipped his head and kissed her. Slow and steady, he held her lips, wallowing in soft caresses. A dream state overwhelmed conscious thought. Rhona upped the pace, finding his tongue and drawing him closer. Being wanted like this was so new. Breathtaking. She didn't conceal how much she desired him and a raging fire burst through his soul.

'I'm not sure I can wait until we get wherever we're going.' She rested her temple on his chest.

'Wait for what?'

'To have all of you.'

'Well, you'll have to. Let's get out of the harbour. We don't want to rock the boat this close to home.'

'Is that a pun?'

He settled himself at the helm. 'You'll see.'

Rhona lounged on one of the sofa benches and flicked him a wink and a smile. 'Then show me what you're made of.'

'Let's just go slow.'

'I meant with the boat.'

'So did I. What else could you possibly mean?' With a smirk, he pulled the tiller and began manoeuvring the boat from the marina.

Chapter Fifteen

Rhona

Rhona's gaze bobbed between Calum and the view. In all her years living on Mull as a youngster, she'd never been on a boat from Tobermory and seeing the island from this point of view was new and interesting. But admiring Calum was better. Her gaze strayed his way. 'Where are you taking me?'

'You told me once, the sea opens up the islands, like it did for your ancestry people.'

Rhona smirked. He'd actually listened to her!

'We could follow their footsteps or boat paths or whatever.' He pushed a button on the digital console in front of him. 'Skirt around the north coast of Mull and out to the Treshnish Isles or we could go straight ahead and cross over to the north tip of Coll.'

'Really? Could we do that? I've never been there.'

'Sure. It's a brilliant cruise. You'll love it. It'll take a couple of hours.'

'Plenty of time to chat then.' She cast him a look. 'And for me to find out all about you.'

His lips curled and he gave a brief headshake. 'Ok. If that's what you want. Or you could take yourself on a tour.'

'Wait until we're away from the land. I'm enjoying seeing places from a different perspective. It brings it home how things worked in the past. For people with boating skills, it was easier getting to Coll on a boat than getting to the other side of the island on foot when there were no roads.'

'Yup, we're living your dream.'

Had the people who lived at Kilnarkie in ancient times arrived in boats from somewhere else? Or were they born on the island to a family who'd lived there through generations? Her romantic ideas kicked in, clashing with cold facts. She wanted to see goodness and cheer in what must have been a harsh and unforgiving life. 'In the Iron Age you and I would have been considered old and wise by now.'

'Yeah?'

'The life expectancy wasn't much over forty, though if you survived infancy, you were in with a fighting chance, but yes, we could be experienced elders by now.'

'And if our families fell out back then, I suppose we'd have gone round their doors and murdered the lot of them.'

'Possibly. Or I'd have been sold to you as a peace offering.'

'Sounds dreadful.'

'I was joking. Though no one knows for sure. Most women probably had their first child around fifteen or sixteen. It was about survival. The sooner they reproduced, the better. I could be almost a grandmother by now.'

'And this is a life you want to relive?'

'It's fascinating. People learned diverse skills and quickly. Societal norms, expectations, and beliefs were so different.'

'You should be a teacher.'

'A lot of archaeologists go into teaching but I still enjoy field work. Just not all the time. I'd like some variety. The last few years I've spent bent over in ditches with very little to show for myself.'

'You've shown me you have lots of talents. You just need to find a job that matches.'

Easier said than done. Rhona pulled up her knees and huddled on the bench. The boat dipped and rose, ploughing through the waves. Early morning sun poked through the clouds like lasers. When they reached open water, Rhona stood and stretched.

'Would you like a turn driving?' Calum glanced over.

'No thanks. I've never loved driving anything.' She sidled over and placed her palms on his shoulders from behind, then bent over and kissed his cheek. 'This is one of the nicest things anyone has ever done for me.'

'You're easily pleased.'

'This is hardly easy. You're giving up time, fuel, and goodness knows what else for me.'

He raised his hand and rubbed it over hers. 'It's not a case of me giving up anything. It's about spending time with somebody I like.'

'Aww.' She leaned in and nuzzled his neck. 'I like you too.' Her arms slipped down and she traced the neat shape of his pecs before holding him close. 'You see, it's possible for a Lamond to like a Matheson.'

'It is. Why don't you look around? Maybe familiarise yourself with the kettle, then a Matheson can have a cup of tea with a Lamond.'

'Oh, haha, you cheeky thing.' She gave him a final squeeze before letting go. 'Ok.'

'I wouldn't mind a green tea.'

'Ooh, a green tea. How very balanced.'

He shook his head and she was sure he'd rolled his eyes. She could have gone directly from the cabin steps but she fancied nosing around first so she exited onto the deck. A sharp gust of wind buffeted her. The sea had changed from the clear blue of the morning to grey and menacing. White foam churned in their wake and Mull grew distant. A thick blanket of cloud descended. Rhona opened the hatch and lowered herself down the ladder.

'Oh my god.' She goggled around. This was the stuff of dreams. Built into the prow was a navy and white striped sofa area with nautical cushions. It must fold out to make a bed. Crossing the highly polished wooden floor, she lounged on the sofa. Wow. This was luxury.

A neat little kitchen area fitted around the ladder, extending until it met the end of the sofa. Every space was used but perfectly neat and uncluttered. She located the sink and kettle, mugs in the cupboard, along with boxes of teabags, a jar of coffee, sugar, even biscuits. He'd made such an effort. She fanned her face, stifling an unexpected wave of emotion. Wow. Overwhelm. This was Calum Matheson. A mini fridge was packed full with supplies. What a romantic. For someone people believed to be a heartless miser, he had a soft side – one that needed to be woken. *So far, so good.* She set the kettle to boil.

Getting the teacups up the ladder without spilling them was a feat in self-management. She wobbled and steadied herself, over and over. Almost all the liquid was in place when she got to the cabin.

'Everything ok?' Calum asked.

'I dread to think how much this boat cost.' Rhona handed him a cup. 'It's totally stunning.'

'Thanks. Blair Robertson helped me fit it out.' He took a sip. 'It's not new, but after the refurbishment, you can't tell.'

'Honestly, Calum, if you said it was brand new, I'd believe you. It's gorgeous.' She cradled her mug, inhaling the warm tea. 'It's got quite windy out there.'

'Yeah. It's coming across us, so it's not the easiest conditions to steer in. I saw there was the chance of stormy weather beyond Coll, this could be the edge of it.'

'Eek.'

'It didn't look like it would reach this far. Then again, in the Hebrides, who can tell?'

'Don't I know it. But it's still safe, isn't it?'

'Yes. These boats can handle a lot of wind. We can moor when we arrive at Coll and see what's what. There's a beautiful little bay where we can drop anchor.'

Calum's words didn't hold any double entendre but Rhona's imagination went haywire. A lonely beach with Calum. Her pulse revved up.

On the horizon, Coll loomed as a long grey shape. It wasn't huge but for two people in a small boat, it was big enough. A couple of hundred people lived there and it was popular with tourists, alongside its neighbour Tiree – the windsurfing capital of Scotland.

The landmass drew closer and Rhona stood to get a better view. Calum skirted the edge of the island until slowly they drew close to a small bay. A serene, white sandy beach rolled out before them.

'Can we get onto that beach?'

Calum pulled a face. 'You're such an adventurer.'

'Is that a yes?'

'We can't get the boat up there. So, if you want to try it, we have to row in with the dinghy and we'll get wet.'

'I have lots of clothes to change into.' She grinned.

'I brought spares too, but I hate getting wet.'

'Why does that not surprise me?'

He rolled his eyes.

'Oh, come on. Please.' She wrapped her arms around his shoulders from behind and put her cheek against his, rubbing against his stubble and breathing in the warmth of his aftershave.

'Ok. But I'll have to find somewhere safe to moor the boat.'

Once he found a place, Rhona scurried out on deck to help. When he was sure they were secure, he untied the dinghy. 'My dad normally does this bit.'

'Shall we take food?'

'Yeah, I've packed a picnic bag. I'll grab it.'

With some wobbling and lots of laughing they managed to offload the supplies and themselves into the dinghy. In the shelter of the bay, the wind wasn't as strong but it still took some muscle power to row to the shore.

With his nose wrinkled, Calum pulled off his shoes and socks. Rhona chuckled as he attempted to roll up his tight jeans. They didn't get further than his ankles. 'It's not that funny. You'll have to do it too.'

'Can't I just sit here and you can pull me out?'

'Oh, anything for you, Miss Lamond.' He hopped out of the boat, splashing into the water. 'Bloody hell, it's cold.' He grabbed the dinghy and dragged it onto the beach. Rhona squealed.

Her hair twisted and tangled as they laid out the picnic mat. She jumped on it before it could blow away. Calum's long narrow feet stretched out in front as they huddled close. Rhona leaned on him and he slipped his arm around her. She glanced up at him and before she could think about anything else, his lips were on her. He laid her back, his fingers tracing the contours of her body from her neck, across her shoulder and onto her breasts. He lingered there for a moment before continuing to her waist. They coiled together. The divine taste of his lips, the wind swirling around and the warmth of the embrace sent Rhona whirling into seventh heaven.

'Are you hungry?' Calum nuzzled her below her ear and she moaned.

'Ravenous.'

'Then let's eat.' He propped himself on his arms and gazed into her eyes.

'Eh, I don't think you got my meaning.'

'Oh, I did.' He winked as he sat up and opened the picnic basket. 'But not out here.'

Rhona stuck close. The wind buffeted around as they ate and her hair tangled with the sandwiches. They kept the food as well covered from the sand as they could. Calum's crisp packet blew off and he leapt to his feet to chase it. When he finally got back, they didn't speak but bundled everything away and shoved it in the dinghy. Rhona gaped at her watch.

'It's half past two.' Where had the day gone? The yacht bobbed a little way off and the sea was a lot more hostile than before.

'Time flies,' Calum said.

'Will we make it back to the boat?' Rhona twisted her hair under her chin as the waves crashed on the shore.

'We bloody better.' Calum shouldered the food bag. 'But we might get wet.' Once Rhona was in the dinghy, he pulled it into the water again and jumped in. His jeans were soaked to the knees. It seemed to take forever battling against the waves. Spray churned over the side almost capsizing them. Rhona screamed.

'Keep going.' Calum jammed his paddle into the water.

Rhona's arms ached by the time they got close enough to the boat to grab the ladder. She grappled the picnic bag on board and Calum climbed up after and hauled up the dinghy. As he secured it to the back, the boat lurched and spray crashed over the deck, soaking him from head to foot. 'Holy hell.' He staggered back. 'Get inside.'

Rhona scurried to the hatch and opened it. Calum descended after her, dripping like a half-drowned rat. He shook himself.

'Let's put the heating on.'

'There's heating?'

'Of course.' Calum fired up a little radiator. 'It's small but it'll do the trick. Give it a few minutes.'

'Will we get home tonight?'

Calum ran his fingers through his drenched hair and screwed up his face. 'I'm not sure I want to attempt it. Not in this wind. We'll bide here for a bit and see if it dies down.'

Rhona chewed on a cuticle. 'I don't mind a storm as long as I'm cosied up safe in my bed. But on a boat?'

'Well...' Calum shrugged off his wet jacket. 'How about a compromise?'

She stopped chewing. 'Go on.'

'I can't change the boat part but we could still get cosied up in bed.'

'Ooh, Mr Matheson, I thought you'd never ask.'

Rubbing water from his face, he grinned. 'I need to dry up a bit first.'

'Or get out of your clothes.'

'All in good time.' He opened a door half hidden behind the ladder.

'What's in there?'

'The toilet. And a sleeping area.'

'Isn't this the bed?' Rhona slapped the built-in seat.

'It's one of them.' He disappeared through the door and Rhona pulled off her coat.

He wasn't gone long. When he returned, he had on sport shorts and a towel across his shoulders. A tight body and shapely pecs greeted her wandering eyes; she followed the thin trail of hair running down the centre of his well-defined abs. She'd snuck a feel of him before through his t-shirt, but all exposed, he was hotter than she'd dreamed.

'Your turn,' he said.

Rhona was still ogling him as she slipped through the door into the narrow corridor. At the end was the alternative sleeping area. Calum's clothes were hanging over a rail. To her right was a door into the dinkiest bathroom area ever. It was moulded to fit the space perfectly. Strip lights reflected off the gleaming white basin surface, toilet and tiny shower cubicle. Rhona had nothing to spruce herself up with but the liquid soap had a fresh enough aroma. The sea air left her hair and skin smelling more amazing than products anyway.

Sitting on the toilet seat, she pulled off her jeans. Her legs trembled and she shivered. Hopefully the bed would be cosy because she was frozen. She emerged in her knickers and her t-shirt pulled low. The jeans were abandoned on the rail in the spare bedroom and she made her way back into the main room, tugging her t-shirt edge as far down as it would go. Calum was straightening out a blanket on top of the bed area.

'That looks amazing. I'm so cold.'

'In you hop then.' He eyed her over and she gave him a shy smile as she shuffled under the covers.

He tossed the towel off his shoulders, and the boat lurched. 'Whoa.' He steadied himself.

He was barely under the covers when she pounced on him, straddling him like she'd done in the tree house, only this time she wasn't planning on being short-changed. His hands slid down her back and settled on her bottom. She crashed her lips onto his, dragging his face close and pouring her soul into the kiss, giving him no reason to doubt how much she wanted this.

With a groan, he nibbled her lip and she squirmed in pleasant surprise. Straightening up, she pulled her t-shirt over her head, letting him get an eyeful, her modesty only covered by her lacy pink bra. He slipped down one strap with his thumb, bent forward and kissed her shoulder.

'You have a tattoo.' He ran a fingertip over it.

'It's the shell. The one I found in Crete.'

'It's cute.' He caressed it and kissed the crook of her neck.

Her head lolled to the side and her hair trailed across her shoulders and arms as she soaked him in. 'I wasn't sure about it.'

'And I wasn't sure about you. But now I am. The shell's beautiful and so are you.' He pushed off her other strap, freeing her. 'Everything about you is beautiful.' He rolled the pads of his thumbs over her breasts and an electric current slammed her stomach. She arched back with a soft cry. His lips found hers and they kissed deeply; their tongues met and more bolts of energy surged through her. His palms were warm and sensual, travelling over her tingling skin. 'I want you so damned much, Rhona.'

'Oh god, I want you too.'

He slipped his hand under the pillow and pulled out a foil packet. 'Best be prepared.'

As he readied himself, Rhona giggled, flicked her hair over her back and plied his muscular shoulder with kisses. This delicious part of his body was so often hidden. He glanced up, shifted his hands to her hips and looked at her.

'I normally find all this so awkward,' he said. 'So much so it's hardly worth it.'

'But not this time?'

'Definitely not.' He sealed his mouth over hers, drawing her into a long drugging kiss. 'There's nowhere I'd rather be.'

The boat lurched, rocking Rhona into an exquisite position on his lap. She draped her arms over his shoulders and leaned her forehead against his. With one arm firmly around her, protecting her from the storm, he used his other to find her sweet spot, teasing her until she closed her eyes and moaned.

'Calum, please,' she muttered. 'I just want…' She whimpered and her lungs burned as she gasped for air.

He drew her close, holding her, kissing her and nuzzling her neck as she crested the wave. His warm palm glided over her back, inside her knickers. He gently moved them to the side and she shifted. Her whole body tingled, nerve ends alight with desire. When he focused his attention back on her breasts, she almost fainted.

Slowly and gently, he nudged his way home and Rhona sank onto him with a moan. This was the moment. A Lamond and a Matheson were bound as one and, god, it was good. Rhona arched back, tipping her head, frantically chasing the peak of ecstasy. Calum's breath was ragged as he ground into her, still finding her sensitive spots with his free palm but keeping a firm hold on her. He was all hers and she was his. She threw her head back further, letting out a cry of delight, drowning as great waves of pleasure flooded her body.

Chapter Sixteen

Calum

Calum rested back on the headboard. Deep contentment dispersed into his veins. Rhona was motionless on his lap, her arms draped over him. Her breathing tickling his neck, making him twitch. She stirred and softly massaged his shoulder, stroking her palms down his back.

Hyper-aware of how much he would usually hate this kind of thing, he kept his eyes closed and relaxed into her hair, allowing himself to enjoy the warmth of her touch. It wasn't bad at all.

'That was good.' Her words fell like a breeze in his ear and he flinched. She soothed him with a gentle kiss and he sighed. Pure bliss.

'It was good,' he murmured. 'Though maybe a bit quick.'

'Sorry, I couldn't wait.'

'Me neither.' He twirled her hair around his finger.

'So it was just right. Exactly what we both needed.' She held him in her firm embrace. 'Next time we can perfect our moves.'

He laughed onto her neck and tightened his hold. 'Deal.' Possibly the best deal he'd ever struck.

Cuddling was growing on him. And fast. There was something so indulgent about it, abandoning the world and enjoying the dreamy heat and comfort. The boat rocked and swayed, and Rhona pulled out of his embrace. Calum released her without a fuss. If anyone knew how horrible it was to be held in a hug they didn't want, it was him.

She smiled at him and grabbed the blanket that had fallen on the floor. 'I'm just getting this. I'm not going away.'

Hoisting it over them, she shuffled in close again. Calum barely had a chance to adjust it to cover them both when she wrapped her arms around him and drew him in tight.

'I'm really not a cuddler, you know.' He put his arms around her and stroked her back. She snuggled in.

'So I see.'

'You're corrupting me.' Right now, he'd do anything she wanted.

'I need a big strong man to keep me safe in the storm.'

He laughed into her soft hair. 'You don't need anything of the sort. But it's definitely a lot warmer like this.'

'Exactly. You're learning.' She squeezed him tighter. 'And cuddling is easy and fun. So, what's not to love?'

'You're right.' He placed a long kiss on her temple. She leaned up and their lips met again. The urgency was quelled and they softly consummated each sublime second. Calum's fingers slipped into her hair and he held her firm, only breaking apart to breathe. 'I wonder what time it is.' He rested his forehead on hers while his lungs caught up. 'I've lost track of everything.'

'We'll be really late back.' Rhona gently kissed his shoulder. 'Maybe I should phone my parents.'

'There won't be reception here,' Calum said. 'Where did you tell them you were going?'

'On a friend's boat. They thought I meant Kirsten. I didn't enlighten them.'

'There's a chance we might not get back tonight. It might be safer to wait it out and go back in the morning. If this is the tail end of that storm, it should blow out overnight.'

'That sounds like an adventure. But how will I let my parents know?'

'Do they need to know?' He looped her hair round his finger again. 'If they think you're with Kirsten, won't they assume you're staying with her?'

'They might. But they'd expect me to send some kind of message. If it gets late and I'm not back, they'll worry.'

'I can radio the coastguard and explain the situation. They might pass on a message.'

'Isn't that abusing the emergency services?'

'I won't call the emergency number, just the local one. I should log our position anyway and let them know we're safe.'

Rhona let out a sigh. 'Ok. Let's do that.'

'It means I'll have to get out of bed.' The corners of his lips turned down. 'Sorry.'

She screwed up her face.

'I don't want to but it's important.'

Her grip slackened and he clambered out. It wasn't freezing but the air outside the bed was nowhere near as cosy as under the covers with Rhona. He ducked into the tiny bathroom and sorted himself out before searching the spare room for the warmest clothes he had with him.

Chilly blasts and stinging rain battered him as he climbed on deck to give the boat a quick check. Every sensation was sharpened after the heat of Rhona's embrace. He shivered, pulling the collar of his Trespass jacket high. *Just a brief interval.* The boat rocked this way and that. He stumbled up to the cabin. His head was light, almost dizzy. He wasn't just working with a Lamond now. Christ, he'd had sex with her. Damn good sex. Nothing like his usual cringy encounters.

He pulled out the radio. *Focus.* His pulse quickened as he waited for a connection. The local coastguards knew his dad. Ron was well known in nautical circles. What Calum was about to tell them might raise eyebrows, but this wasn't a time for nonsense. He gritted his teeth as he puzzled out how to word it without it sounding too suspicious.

He recognised the voice as soon as the man spoke. Calum relayed their coordinates and explained the situation in brief.

'I've got you on the tracker,' the coastguard said. 'And are you safe?'

'Yes, we're fine at the moment. We're in a sheltered area and we've got enough supplies to keep us going for a couple of days if necessary.'

'Great. But if anything changes, let us know immediately.'

'Listen...' He swallowed. 'You couldn't do a favour for me, could you?'

'What's that?'

'Rhona Lamond is on the boat with me, she's doing an archaeological trip.' He cleared his throat. 'We expected to be back this evening, so her parents won't know where she is. You couldn't get a message to Alister Lamond, could you? I have his number here.'

'No worries, Calum. I'll give him a call and let him know. And remember, if the situation changes, call us straight away.'

'I will. Thanks.'

He signed off and stowed the radio, then slumped into the seat. That coastguard would know about the Matheson/ Lamond feud. He'd been the consummate professional but how could he let Rhona's family know she was safe without saying who she was with?

Back below deck, Calum dropped onto the bed and ran his hand over his hair. 'I'm sorry, I can't guarantee he won't say who you're with.'

Rhona sucked her lip. 'They'll probably panic even more if they think I'm stuck out here with you.'

'Yeah. Sorry about that.' He peered up at her.

'There's not much we can do about it.'

'Here.' Calum patted the bed beside him and Rhona huddled in. 'I could get used to this cuddling thing.' He gently rocked her in his arms and they sat in silence for some minutes. Rain bounced off the deck above and spattered the tiny windows. The boat lurched.

'Calum.' Rhona's voice was little more than a whisper. 'What if we come clean? We could tell them the truth.'

'I was thinking that too. But how? What if our families disown us?'

'Mine would.'

'Exactly. Could you live with that?'

'No. And it's not just that. They'd find ways to hurt you even more than they do now. They'd never trust your motives. My dad is always talking of ways he can bring you down but so far, he's only done petty things. I'm scared he'd go all out to get you.'

Calum traced the shell tattoo with his fingertips. 'I expect you're right. But I'm more worried about them cutting you off. You've always been so special to them.'

'Ha. Their baby girl.'

'Exactly. And we don't know what'll happen with us. You could leave any day.'

She increased her grip on him, the heat seeping into his cold veins and rushing to his core. How could he bear to lose this?

'Maybe we should keep things under wraps until we're clearer on where we want to take this.' As the words flowed, his heart withered. He wanted to believe it was going somewhere special. Shout it from the rooftops. But instead, he had to sweep it under the carpet. 'Let's not make any rash decisions.'

'Ok... Well, only one.' She straddled him again and wrapped her arms around his neck. 'I'm not done with you yet.'

His grin flickered and he let it loose. 'We've got all night, so let's not rush this time.'

This was a gift he wanted to unwrap slowly, savouring every hot second. After Rhona's insatiable desire the first time round, she'd calmed too and they spent a lazy hour of exploration, letting their fingers, mouths and tongues discover the perfect spots, delivering an oxytocin overload to his system.

Cuddling was his new favourite thing and as the evening rolled on, he was happy to lie wrapped in Rhona's arms chatting and kissing. The emotional intimacy as powerful as the physical. Eventually, they dragged themselves up and had some food but it was quick. The room had warmed up, so it wasn't unpleasant out of the bed, but it was nowhere near as enjoyable as being snuggled under the covers, enfolded in each other's arms, so close they were one – in body and soul.

'Just as well I don't get seasick,' Rhona said as the boat rocked.

'Would you have agreed to come on a boat trip if you did?'

'No. That would have been silly.' She tightened the fleece blanket she'd lifted from atop the duvet around her shoulders. 'Let's get back to bed.'

'I'll wash up first. I like to keep a tidy ship.'

'Why does that not surprise me?'

'You'll thank me in the morning.'

'Ok, let me help.'

'You're not exactly dressed for it.' Calum had pulled on his shorts; Rhona hadn't bothered with anything but the blanket.

She let it drop. 'I'll show you I can work just as well like this.'

'I'm not sure I can though.' He scanned over her sensational curves.

They cleared up, Rhona distracting him completely. The boat swayed and he steadied himself as he put away the crockery.

'I hope we're going to be safe.' Rhona ran a dishcloth around the rim of a mug.

'Me too. I don't think I'll get much sleep. I'll be wide awake listening for water getting in.'

'That's not why you won't be sleeping.' Rhona winked.

'Incorrigible, you are.' Calum put the last plate away, then grabbed her hand and pulled her close, dipping in to kiss her cheek.

She clamped his butt and held him tight against her. 'There's no keeping a good man down, is there?' She waggled her eyebrows.

'Let's get in.' He jumped under the covers. Rhona followed on the other side and soon they were cosied up again. He closed his eyes and nuzzled into her hair. 'If we're going to drown at least I get to die happy.'

She prodded his shoulder. 'That's not funny.'

He tugged her as close as possible and kissed her forehead. 'Let's see if we manage any sleep.'

Rhona circled her fingertips across the planes of his back. 'I'm definitely not tired.'

'Christ, you're high maintenance.'

'Aren't I just.'

He rolled her over, shifting on top. Her skin was soft and warm, inviting him to come and indulge. He showered her with kisses, a lifetime's worth. Ones he'd been saving forever until the right person came along, and here she was, right here.

They rocked together with the boat, upping the tempo, then slowing as the wind came to a crescendo around them. When every ounce of ecstasy had been milked from his system, he flopped onto her, shattered enough to sleep for a week.

Calum opened his eyes. Rhona was spooned in his arms and the boat was still. He sat up and listened for a few moments. Gently prising himself from her, he slipped to the bathroom, before giving the boat a quick check, listening for rushing water.

He pulled on a t-shirt and his sports shorts and headed outside. The murky sea and the nearby island were visible in the early morning haze. He checked the time on his phone. It was just before four. They would leave in a few hours.

Wanting to make the most of this time with Rhona, he shuffled behind her, warming himself on her soft skin. She moaned and snuggled in. Slowly, he drifted back to sleep.

The next time he opened his eyes, someone was kissing his throat, then his chest. He gave a soft moan. *No one has ever wanted me this much.* Did he deserve it? There must be something amiss if a Lamond was making him feel this good... *Too damn good.* Not after what he'd done to Arran. None of the objections he'd voiced last night were as important as that one. He wasn't a safe man to be around. They were right to hate him. What if he snapped like that again and hurt her? 'No,' he groaned.

'You want me to stop?' Rhona looked up, her blue irises twinkling in the pale light.

'No.' The word was barely out when she kissed him again, starting on the centre of his ribcage, working her way towards his navel.

Shit. Help. He never wanted to hurt her. Not Rhona. He threaded his fingers into her hair and his eyelids dropped as she worked her way further down his body, kissing and stroking him in places no one had ever kissed him before. Conscious thought drifted away and he tumbled into paradise.

They didn't get out of bed as early as he'd imagined.

'Does the shower work?' Rhona asked.

'Of course, why?'

'Just checking.'

'Well, if it's broken, you could try skinny dipping instead. I'll sit on deck and watch.'

Rhona chucked a cushion at him. 'If I'm skinny dipping, so are you.'

'Shower it is then. There's no danger I'm swimming in there.'

'You're so funny. Can I make that another mission? To get you skinny dipping?'

'Definitely not.'

After he'd washed and put on clean clothes, he started the boat's engine. The storm had cleared the air and sun split the sky. Rhona dotted around on deck, coming in and out now and then to chat. Her company was like her cuddles. It wrapped up his heart and warmed it. He was the most special man in the universe.

After a couple of hours, Mull loomed into view and Calum followed the coast towards Tobermory. Rhona opened the door from the deck and threw herself onto the sofa bench with a low groan. Calum glanced over. Her face was pinched and drawn.

'Is everything ok?'

'We've got reception again.' She grimaced at her phone. 'About a hundred messages have come in from my mum and dad. They're furious with you and want to know if I'm still alive.'

Calum huffed out a sigh. 'No surprise then.'

'What should I tell them?' Rhona's eyes pleaded with him.

What indeed? If they knew the truth, they'd be more than furious. They'd wrestle him from the boat, beat him with heavy objects, tie a weight to his leg and fling him off the harbour. Melodramatic maybe, but accurate as hell. 'Say I took you to see an archaeological site or something. That's what I told the coastguard.' He stared forward. He'd known this couldn't last but the truth plunged into his stomach like a shard of ice. They could never be anything without rupturing their families.

Rhona typed a message. 'Ok, I'll tell them that and say we're almost back, so they can stop freaking out.'

Just over half an hour later, Calum steered the boat into the marina towards its berth. His blood ran cold. 'Oh no.' Standing quayside were Alister and Judy Lamond, arms folded, faces red. 'Did you ask your parents to pick you up?'

'No.'

'Well, they're here.'

'What?' Rhona jumped to her feet. 'Oh my god, Calum. I'm sorry. I better get my stuff ready. They'll want me to go with them straightaway.' She ran from the cabin and thumped onto the deck. Calum navigated the boat in, doing his best not to make eye contact with the two people marching along the wooden jetty.

'Fuck.' He had to get out to secure the ropes. 'This is just great.' If only the sea would part and let him slip away.

As he left the cabin, he scanned down and caught Alister's glower. Fury was etched into his brow. Judy was so like her daughter in looks, it was as if an older version of Rhona was frowning up at him, pursing her lips and giving him the evils. He bowed his head and went straight for the rope.

'Where's Rhona?' Alister shouted.

Calum gripped the rope tightly; the fibres burned into his skin. *Stay calm. For Christ's sake, stay calm. For Rhona's sake, keep calm.* He leapt onto the jetty. *Do not overreact or say anything stupid.* Taking the rope's coiled end, he wound it around the bollard. 'She's just coming.' He didn't look at them.

'Why the hell did you think it was ok to take her to another island when a storm was forecast?'

Calum wound the rope carefully and slowly. 'That's not what happened.' Blood rushed to his head.

'Clearly it is. Either that or you didn't check the forecast. Either way, it was a dreadful error of judgement. She could have died.'

'There was no chance of that.' The words snapped before Calum could stop them.

'I don't know what you did to her to make her go with you but if anything has happened to her, I will not rest until you're rotting in a jail cell.'

'Where you should have been for the last sixteen years,' Judy said.

Calum kept his eyes low, beating down the boiling rage threatening to erupt.

'Here she is.' Judy pushed onto tiptoes. 'Good god, are you all right?'

'Of course I am.' Rhona's sweet voice placated the anger in Calum for a split second.

'Thank god,' Alister muttered. 'And as for you.' He waggled his finger.

Calum straightened up and met his glare.

'Stay away from her if you know what's good for you.' He stalked off.

Judy thrust her arm around Rhona's shoulder and dragged her away. Neither looked back. Calum jumped on the boat and descended below deck, sinking onto the bed. No surprise at the outcome. *How could I have thought things would be different?* With a huge effort he stood, bracing himself on the worktop. His lungs spasmed like they were filling with water. After such a wonderful twenty-four hours, now all he wanted to do was tie the anchor to his foot and jump overboard.

Chapter Seventeen

Rhona

'Mum, let go of me. I'm fine.' Rhona pulled herself free of Judy's grip on her shoulder. Instinct clawed at her to look back and wave to Calum but she mastered herself. It wasn't worth it. Her parents would flip and they both seemed on the verge of a Matheson-induced breakdown as it was. She couldn't risk them taking it out on him and reporting him for goodness knew what.

'Are you sure you're all right?' Judy scanned her over from top to toe.

'Yes. Why wouldn't I be?' *What age am I? Twelve?* Judy dragged her further along the jetty away from the Dawn Treader. The wooden slats creaked underfoot. They were treating her like a child they'd rescued from a mad kidnapper, not a woman who'd had the night of her life with a man she was crazy about.

'He didn't try anything on, did he?' Judy lowered her voice to a hiss.

Rhona shook her head. Words failed. There was barely a move they hadn't tried last night, but how could she articulate that without her dad turning back, leaping on the boat and throwing Calum overboard? Or her mum taking her to the police station and reporting him for assault, then marching her to a doctor to be examined both physically and mentally. 'It was just business.'

Alister glared at her. 'Why in hell's name were you doing business with him? What sort of business? Is he forcing you into something?'

'No. He needed an archaeologist to do some work on his land. I agreed to do it, but I didn't tell you because I knew you'd be cross.'

'Cross?' Alister cracked his knuckles. 'Of course I'm cross. He's a violent and highly aggressive man. You're lucky he didn't attack you.'

'Dad, he really isn't.'

'You have no idea what you're talking about.' Alister's neck was red and blotchy. 'He can talk the talk. It's how he's escaped the law all these years, but I've seen the evidence. I know what he's capable of and I'll never forget it. He almost killed your brother when he was seventeen. Who's to say what he might do when he snaps.'

'I've never seen that side to him.'

'Just as well,' Judy said. 'If he ever lays a finger on anyone in this family again, I'll make sure he's locked up and the key thrown away. He got off lightly before. I always said we should have pressed charges.'

'Yes. I wish we had. I should have listened to you.' Alister patted Judy's back. 'I thought remorse would get the better of him, but it hasn't. He's got more and more arrogant. He's conned his way into money and scammed people all over the island. He shows no respect for anyone and is nothing but a blight on our community.'

Rhona massaged a slow circle around her temples. Her heart was crying but she made sure nothing showed on her face. She neutralised her expression, temporarily numbing her senses. Later the pain dams would burst but not here. It was like being a child again. Her sisters screaming at each other, threatening to cut each other's hair, or shave the other's eyebrows off if they didn't do whatever. Rhona powerless to do anything other than wish it would stop. Like now.

'Where is the land you've been working on?' Judy asked.

'At Kilnarkie.'

'Kilnarkie? Near the old churchyard?'

'Yes.'

'I never wanted him to have that land,' Alister said. 'He'll ruin it with one of his developments. That's a beautiful, rugged spot and it doesn't need any ridiculous buildings on it. If you're working for him, make sure you create as much hell for him as possible. Though I'd much prefer it if you handed in your notice and good riddance.'

'I've finished the work now.'

'So, why were you in the boat with him?'

'I told you, he took me to Coll. There was a site there I wanted to see.' How the lies tripped off her tongue. Her heart shrivelled. Tears threatened. The only person who could stop them was Calum. She wanted to be back in his embrace, enjoying the soothing strokes of his palms, the strong hold of his arms and the gentle comfort of his kisses.

As soon as she got into the car, she pulled out her phone. Her parents were still busy tearing Calum and the Mathesons to shreds. Rhona's chest ached like she was stuck under an iron gate. She typed out a message.

RHONA: OMG! I am soooo sorry about that. I hope this doesn't ruin everything. I still want to see you again. I miss you already. Please let this be ok. XXXX

She hit send and clutched the phone tight, hoping for an immediate response. The words were true but the situation was impossible. Her parents' reaction was a taster of what she could expect if they found out the truth. Their wrath could erupt into serious damage if this got out. Calum hadn't done anything illegal, had he? But Alister was a smart man and could probably twist facts. Could they retrospectively press charges for his attack on Arran? Things like that came up on the news all the time. How could she stand that on her conscience if they had him jailed?

The scenery whirred by in a blur of green forests and hills. Was Calum violent? Since knowing him, she couldn't believe it. He'd never shown any tendency to violence. Yet she'd seen what he'd done to Arran. Couldn't they forgive him now? She knew the answer. She laid back her head, scrunching her eyes tight. Why had he attacked Arran in the first place? Her dad always made it sound like an unprovoked attack but what if it wasn't? Could it have been over the girlfriend he'd mentioned in the tree house? Had he been so enraged with Arran stealing her that he'd beaten him up? At school he hadn't appeared violent either. If anything, it was the opposite. He'd always seemed quiet, withdrawn and didn't stand out one way or another.

No messages came in. Rhona paced like a caged animal, prowling around her parents' house unable to settle at anything. The dig was done and the report complete so she couldn't distract herself with work. Alister and Judy huddled in the kitchen muttering to each other and Rhona couldn't listen to what she knew would be schemes to hurt Calum. Couldn't they leave him alone? She checked her phone every few seconds. Still no messages. *Why doesn't he reply?* Was he having second thoughts? Could she blame him? The tug in her tummy forced her not to believe any of it. It couldn't be over. Not yet.

The following day, she worked on the reconstruction. An email came in with the pricing details. Would Calum still want it? He'd pushed her to do it but would he shut her down now? Still, it gave her a reason to talk to him – other than just wanting to.

During the day he'd be at his office or out and about at his properties. She didn't want to disturb him while he was working.

But with a little bit of snooping, she found his home address on one of the dig site official documents.

Judy narrowed her eyes when Rhona asked to borrow the car.

'I need to deliver something to Kirsten.' Rhona fixed her smile.

'Just don't be too late,' Judy said. 'You know how much we worry.'

Rhona recognised the modern block of flats in Tobermory. It was unmistakable and easily the most Calum-like place in the town, kitted out with huge window walls and balconies. Quite the place for a bachelor pad.

She buzzed the secure entry system and bounced on her feet.

'Hello.' His voice crackled through the speaker.

'It's Rhona, can I come up?'

Silence.

She fiddled with her nails, staring at the keypad on the door, willing it to unlock. Finally, the door clicked, and she snatched it open before he had the chance to change his mind. She took the stairs two at a time until she came face to face with a large number. She was about to knock when the door opened. Calum leaned on the frame dressed in his gym shorts and a tight vest top. Beads of sweat covered his brow. Working out? The masculine pheromones set her nerve ends tingling.

His eyebrows joined in a flat line and his jaw set but when he spoke his words were gentle. 'What is it, Rhona?'

'I wanted to talk to you. You didn't reply to my message.'

He stared at his feet and rubbed his forehead. 'I'm sorry. I should have. I just didn't know what to say. I can't set your mind at ease or change anything about the situation, it is what it is.'

'Can I come in?'

He gazed at her for a few seconds then put out his arm. She stepped inside. The second the door clicked shut, she flung her arms around his neck.

'Whoa.' He returned her hug though his body was rigid. 'I'm really sweaty.'

'I don't care. I missed you so much. Don't you get it?'

'Of course I do. And I missed the hell out of you too but it doesn't change anything.'

She clung to him. 'What have you been doing?'

'Practising for the karate competition. I'm so out of it. I need to get back in shape.'

She traced the contours of the muscles on his shoulders and upper arms with the pad of her thumb. Definitely not out of shape.

'Is there someone else here?' She slowly loosened her grip and stared at him.

'No, I've got a grappling dummy that I practice on.'

'Is that like a blow-up doll?'

His answering expression made her laugh. 'No.' He led her into a room with mats on the floor, weights, a punchbag suspended from the ceiling and a weird-looking, human-shaped dummy thing on a stand.

'A blow-up doll and your very own dungeon. Why, Mr Matheson, I didn't realise that was the kink you were into.'

'Shut up. Or I'll teach you a few throws.'

'Does it involve me landing on my back and you jumping on top of me?'

'Possibly. That would make a change from the last time. I seem to remember you being the one jumping on top of me.'

She giggled and poked his arm. 'You see, this is why I miss you.'

He slung his arm around her shoulder and kissed her forehead. She closed her eyes and soaked it up. 'If you think of a way to make it work, then let me know.'

'Let's do what you suggested. We see each other but don't shout about it.' Cupping her palm around his cheek, she pulled him in for a kiss. He snaked his arm behind her and edged her backwards until she met something solid. Pressing his other hand flat on the wall beside her head, he pushed up against her, still kissing her. His raw masculinity drove her to bursting point.

'Ok.' Their noses touched as he spoke. 'I'd like you to stay for a while but I need to practise. The competition is in three weeks and I've been so lax. It's hard to practise when there aren't many people on the island to do it with.'

'If you really want to throw me around, let's do it.'

He let out a laugh and pressed his forehead against hers. 'I'm a black belt, remember. I'm definitely not going to throw you around, but thanks for the offer.'

'How about I cheer you on instead then? I can pretend I have pompoms.'

'What a vision. But I like it.' He dipped in and kissed her again. 'Watch if you like.'

Rhona settled on a mat to watch him thump the dummy, cringing as he kicked and beat it mercilessly.

It developed into a routine over the next few weeks. To stop her parents getting too suspicious, Rhona chose two nights and stuck to them, pretending she was attending a yoga class in Tobermory with Kirsten. Judy didn't ask any questions and Alister barely lifted his head from his book when she told them she was going, so she assumed they suspected nothing.

She dressed in her workout clothes: black and grey leggings and a matching crop top. Very authentic.

'How about you teach me some basic moves?' she asked Calum. He gave her the once over.

'Your outfits are so distracting.' He dusted off his palms.

'How come?' She glanced down. 'I thought I looked pretty good.'

'You look bloody hot, that's the problem.' He slipped his arms around her waist and pulled her close. 'Let's fight it out.'

'Seriously? You sure you got the right F word?'

'For now.'

'So... You'll actually teach me?'

'A few basic moves, yeah.'

She jumped into a fake Ninja pose, crossing her arms in front of her. 'Then can I take you down?'

'Er... No.' He raised an eyebrow and put his hands on his hips, opening his broad shoulders to their fullest. 'Well, you could try...'

She giggled. 'Ok, maybe not.' She paid close attention as he demonstrated a few basic punches, copying them as best she could, then attempting to throw some punches while he blocked her.

'This is so much fun.' She launched another punch at him. He blocked her and stuck his foot out to trip her but stopped.

'Concentrate. You nearly ended up on your back.'

'It won't be the first time.' She winked.

He smirked and dusted his shoulder before squaring up to her again.

'Can I come to the competition with you? I've watched the practises. I should be there to cheer you on.'

'I doubt it'll be the most riveting day for you. It'll be a lot of sitting around and there's every chance I'll get knocked out in round one. I'm not kidding, I'm out of practise.'

'Please.' She took hold of his vest straps and pulled him close. 'I want to. You're my guy and I want to cheer you on.'

'Ok.' He bent in and kissed her. 'I suppose if we're on the mainland, there's less chance of people seeing us out together.'

'Exactly. We can be free. I can hold your hand in public.' She'd shout it around town, *I love Calum Matheson*, if she dared. Her heart fluttered like hundreds of butterflies had taken it over. She did love Calum. If they split now, it would break her, but was there a solution that would let her keep both him and her family?

Whenever she saw Calum, she threw affection at him, with hugs, kisses, sex, positive words, even just smiles. It was her only outlet. At home, she suppressed her feelings, hardly daring to speak in case she betrayed what was going on in her head.

'It's a nightmare at home,' she told Calum as she watched his latest practice. 'Arran's coming back this weekend.'

'Hmpf.' Calum threw a hefty punch at the dummy.

Rhona groaned and slid down the wall, tugging her knees to her chest. If Arran found out what she was doing here... She covered her face. *I can't bear to think about it.* If he met Calum and discovered what was going on, they might try murdering each other again. Arran definitely wouldn't take the news lying down. If he thought Calum had defiled his little sister, god knew what he might do.

'Mum's scrubbed the house so the carpet's almost threadbare and the paint's been taken off the walls. She's obsessed with cleaning.' Rhona splayed her fingers to watch Calum thrust kick the dummy. 'You'd think the bloody queen was visiting.'

'No offence, but he always thought he was royalty the way he strutted around.'

'Did he? He always looked out for me.'

'Yeah...' Calum adjusted his waistband. 'Listen, I need an early night tonight.' He smacked his fist into the dummy's torso. 'A good sleep is important before a competition.'

'Ok.' Rhona dragged herself to her feet. 'And you'll pick me up tomorrow?'

'Bright and early. What have you told your parents this time?'

She sighed. 'That I'm going mainland shopping.'

'And they believe you?'

'Yup.'

'Good, so I'll see you tomorrow then.'

He kissed her goodnight, lingering on her bottom lip before pulling away. Rhona moaned. Saying goodbye even overnight was a wrench. But tomorrow, they'd be together. Alone and free on the mainland. She almost skipped down the stairs.

Chapter Eighteen

Calum

The car door opened and Rhona jumped in. *Wow.* Calum's jaw dropped. She looked spellbinding in a white gypsy top and floaty scarf. Before he could voice his appreciation, her arms snaked around his neck and she kissed him. He tasted her sweet lip gloss; her smile pressed against him. Whatever happened at the competition didn't matter if he had this. Except he didn't. Not really.

'Let's go.' He broke away, running his finger down her cheek. Rhona sat back, her complexion rosy and her lips pink and shimmering. 'You look gorgeous.'

She blinked, beaming.

'But you didn't have to dress up. It's not televised or anything. Not that I don't appreciate it.' He patted her thigh as he pulled off.

'Any excuse. I spend most of my life in mucky jeans so this is a nice change.'

'You're a knockout, Miss Lamond. Whatever you wear.'

'Oh, Mr Matheson. You're making me blush. What a charmer you are.'

'Just telling the truth.' The empty road twisted before them towards the village of Dervaig. They passed the road to Will's house and Calum made a mental note to drop in and see him sometime. He'd woefully neglected him and everybody since Rhona took over his world.

He'd already travelled the serpentine-like road between Tobermory and Dervaig to fetch Rhona and seen only a couple of cars. This time, he turned onto the road that crossed the island diagonally, heading towards the ferry port. The sun glowed behind the layer of clouds, promising a warm day once it broke through, not that he'd see it. He'd be either competing or hanging round the sports centre. Hopefully Rhona wouldn't find it too dull. The chance he'd be knocked out early on was high and that would give them plenty of free time to spend the day together.

'When we get to the ferry, I have to nip in and see my mum and dad,' he said. 'Mum messaged me last night, she's got something for me.'

'Ok.' Rhona smoothed her long skirt.

'I'll walk over after I put the car in lane, if you don't mind waiting.'

'Of course, that's fine.'

He passed her a smile full of emotions he wished he could put into words, things he wasn't sure how to articulate even to himself. He didn't want a second without her in his life. Her twinkling eyes met his. *She understands. I'm sure.* Turning his gaze back to the road, he drove on, his chest buoyant and his head light.

Several cars, vans and trucks were already in the ferry queue and Calum followed the attendant's direction into Lane B.

He dragged on the handbrake, flipped open his wallet and pushed in the tickets. 'Best keep them safe, I don't want to lose them for the way back. I'll jog over to Mum and Dad's and see what they've got for me.'

'Is it your birthday?'

'No, that was two months ago.' He bent in and kissed her cheek. 'I won't be long. I'll leave the keys.'

He crossed the loading lane onto the promenade that ran around beside the bus park. His parents' house was already in view as he took the shore path. Strolling along with his hands in his pockets, he glanced back. The car was out of view. How things had changed. Calum Matheson had left his vehicle at the mercy of a Lamond. He rounded the corner, smirking, and hopped up to the gate. Knocking was a formality, and after one rap, he pushed the door open.

'Hello, is anybody home?'

'Ah, Calum, aw' right, son.' Ron came out the kitchen, pulling a jacket onto his bulky frame. 'Mum's just hanging up the washing and we'll be ready.'

'Ready for what?'

'Oh, I forgot, she hasn't told you. We're coming to watch.'

'You're what?'

'Aye, she wanted to surprise you. Curse my big mouth but no harm done. You'd have found out ten seconds from now anyway.'

Heat rose up Calum's neck. 'Honestly, Dad, there's no need for you to watch.'

'We know that.' Ron clapped him on both arms and beamed. 'But we want to support our lad.'

'No, seriously. It'll be deadly dull. Can't we go for dinner another time instead?'

'Oh, stop it. Do you think your old mum and dad mind spending a day with their lad?'

'Of course I don't.' He sank his teeth into the inside of his lip. *This is all I need.* 'Thing is, Dad, I've already got someone... a friend, coming with me.'

'Wonderful.' Ron grinned. 'We can all cheer for you. Who is it? Will?'

'No,' Calum muttered. 'She's... um...'

Ron's eyebrows shifted high up his forehead towards his shiny bald scalp. '*She?* Ooh, son, you kept that one quiet.'

'Yeah, exactly. So, you see, it could get awkward.'

'Oh, so she's a proper girlfriend.' Ron clapped Calum's arms. 'Well done.'

'No, Dad. Not that.' His neck must be beetroot by now; it burned right to his ears. He didn't want to deny her, but how could he confess?

'Ah, there you are.' Anne bustled in and grabbed her coat. 'Has Dad told you the surprise?'

'Yes.'

'It's exciting, isn't it?' She bounded up and pinched his cheeks. 'I haven't watched you compete for such a long time. I can't wait to cheer you on.'

'Mum.'

'He's taking a girlfriend,' Ron said. 'I'm not sure he wants us going along too.'

'That's not what I said.'

Anne's face fell. 'A girlfriend.'

'A friend, yes, and she happens to be a girl... a woman.' This was getting worse. He pinched the bridge of his nose.

'Surely she won't mind us being there,' Anne said.

'We'll be on our best behaviour.' Ron saluted, crossed himself, then did another thing that was a cross between Scout's honour and some Vulcan sign.

Calum squeezed his eyes shut. What a disaster.

'That's the boat coming now.' Anne took hold of his arm. 'I'm sure she'll be happy to have company. Watching these things on your own is boring. I'd love to meet her.'

Calum's insides were slowly being ripped apart. How could he stop them coming when they were doing it for his benefit? Normally he'd have been touched by the gesture. But his mum would recognise Rhona in a flash. And what then? Could he message her? Warn her. He fumbled for his phone as Ron locked up.

'So, tell us about the girl,' Anne said. 'What kind of friend is she if she's not a girlfriend?'

'Look, Mum, it's complicated.'

'Don't sweat it, son.' Ron laughed, slapping his back. 'We can always walk onto the ferry and meet you at the sports centre if you prefer and we don't have to sit with her if it's a problem.'

'Are we that embarrassing?' Anne asked.

'We are.' Ron chuckled.

Calum strode ahead. *Slow down.* His subconscious nudged him. *Postpone this meeting as long as possible.* But the boat was almost in and once it was it was amazing the speed it offloaded. He needed to be at the car ready to drive on.

'No, you're not,' he said. And he meant it. He wasn't embarrassed by them. What was making him sweat was the woman standing beside his car. Even from this distance, he spied her leaning on the open door, her blonde hair flowing in the wind. Her eyes roamed around searching for him and any second now they'd find him... and not just him. Had she got his message? He crossed his fingers at his side.

'Is that the girl?' Ron squinted towards the line of cars. 'What a looker. Well done.' He slapped Calum's shoulder.

'Dad, please.'

'Isn't that the Lamond girl?' Anne's voice cut through the air over the ferry's rumbling engine and the passing traffic.

Calum loosened his collar. 'Yes.'

'You're dating one of the Lamonds?' Ron's smile sagged and fell.

'Did I say I was dating her?'

'No, but—'

'She's working for me and this is...'

'What?' Anne grabbed his arm, her expression equally as flat as Ron's.

'Look, be nice, ok. She's not her parents and she's not her brother.'

'After what they did to you?' Anne shook her head. 'In fact, what they've done to our family for the last sixteen years. They've never stopped making up lies about us. Not a day goes by when I don't hear something in the shop they've said about you.'

'Please. Don't drag her into this.'

Rhona's eyes were always wide and round but they seemed to pop out of her face when she spotted them approaching. She swayed on the spot and gaped. Where to look? He fought to hold her gaze but couldn't. By the time they reached her, she'd closed the door and was standing outside the car. She clamped her lip under her teeth and fiddled with the edge of her top.

'Um...' Calum flexed his hands. 'This is my mum and dad, and this is Rhona.' He briefly glanced at her. 'I, um, well, they're coming too. They wanted to surprise me.'

'Oh.' Rhona swallowed and tucked her hair behind her ears. 'Nice to meet you.'

'And you.' Ron barely looked at her.

'I suppose we should get in.' Anne marched to the far side of the car. 'I guess we'll both be in the backseat.'

Calum closed his eyes and slowly inhaled. When he opened them, Rhona was staring at him and his parents were in the car. 'I sent you a message. I'm sorry, I didn't know they were going to do this.'

'My phone's in the car. I didn't check it.'

He moved closer. 'If you'd rather not come, I'll understand.'

'I want to. For you.'

'This could go horribly wrong.' He traced his thumb down her arm. 'I don't want you to get hurt.'

'Is that likely?'

'Emotionally. They're not mean people but...'

'I know. The history.'

'Exactly.'

'Let's go with it for now. If things go pear-shaped, I'll walk back to the ferry and come home.' She pushed up and kissed his cheek.

'Ok.' He strode around to his side of the car, hyper-aware Rhona had kissed him. His parents would have noticed. Bang went the story they were just friends.

He peered at them in the mirror but they weren't looking back. Instead, they passed a loaded glance between them. Nobody spoke. Calum had never known them to be so quiet. The atmosphere was like smog. As they descended into the ship's dark hull and parked the car, the gloom closed in around him. He was stuck between two warring factions. And soon he'd have to abandon Rhona. All the joy of having her with him was being sucked away.

They gathered their jackets and headed up the steep stairs in the ship's centre onto the main deck. The silence was now grating. Anne marched directly from the stairs to the little shop and busied herself looking around.

'I might go for a walk about,' Ron said.

Anne checked up. 'I'll come with you.' She squinted at Calum but he gave a brief headshake.

Once they'd gone, he let out a long low whistle. 'I'm sorry.'

Rhona threw her arms around his neck and he pulled her close. 'It's ok, really.' Her palms soothed his shoulders, rubbing gentle strokes along them. 'I want to support you. I know this will be awkward, but I want to try.'

He buried his face in her hair, inhaling the floral conditioner and drawing comfort from it. 'I just don't want to hurt anyone.'

'You won't.' She planted a kiss on his cheek.

They broke apart and wordlessly agreed to walk out on deck. The sun had burned its way through the clouds and the sky was as blue as Rhona's eyes. Calum leaned on the rails. The karate competition was now the least of his concerns. Losing early was the best plan; they could go home. Except he'd booked a later ferry. They'd planned to spend all day in Oban, shopping, walking, dining – anything. Passing the time in Rhona's company was the most important thing. Now it was hours and hours of torture to get through. He slipped his hand over hers and held it as they leaned side by side.

They were almost in Oban when Ron and Anne found them. Calum and Rhona were still resting on the rail hand in hand, neither speaking much. Calum took comfort just from her being there. Now he was the adjudicator stuck between the three people he loved most in the world.

'I'm going to the loo.' Rhona gave Calum a little pat and smiled briefly at Ron and Anne.

Calum stared forward as the heavy door clunked shut.

'Calum, what's this all about?' Anne asked.

He focused on the small rocky islets at the head of the bay and didn't answer.

'I know she's not her parents or her brother, but she's still one of them.'

'Please, Mum.'

'I'm not judging. I'm just curious.' She grasped his arm. 'I can't bear the idea of you being hurt again. She looks like a nice person and maybe she is, but Arran was exactly the same. He was your best friend for years and look what happened.'

'But she's not Arran and she's nothing like him. Do you think I've entered into this lightly or without any thought?' He rubbed his forehead, willing this to resolve itself painlessly.

'Maybe you know best.'

'I don't know if I do or not, but please, don't make it any harder.'

'So, she is your girlfriend?' Ron waggled his eyebrows.

Calum stared ahead. What to say? Nothing would make it right.

'It all makes me very anxious,' Anne said. 'I don't trust any of them.'

A slight cough behind made them spin around. Rhona stood with her lips pressed together, her gaze moving from person to person. Before anyone could speak, the announcer's voice burst from the Tannoy, telling them to return to their vehicles. Calum positioned himself between Rhona and his parents as they made their way downstairs.

What the hell would they do once they got to the competition? Would they sit beside each other? Maybe they shouldn't. Should he suggest they sit apart?

He drove off the boat and straight for the sports centre. The car park was over half full and Calum pulled into a space near the back of the building. A yellow sandwich-board sign pointed to the competitors' entrance.

'I have to go this way,' he said. 'I've messaged you all my competitor's code so you can get a spectator's badge.' He lifted his kitbags out the boot and slammed it. Ron pulled him in for a hug.

'Knock 'em out, son.' He slapped his back hard. 'We'll be shouting you on.'

'Thanks, Dad.' He went to his mum and hugged her. 'I love you, Mum. Thanks for coming.'

'Aw, you'll make me cry, you big softy.' She clung to him. 'Whatever happens in there, you're still my best boy.'

'Mum, if you want to sit on your own, it's ok, really,' he whispered.

'Don't worry, we're all adults, we'll be fine.' She kissed his cheek.

Rhona gave Calum a weak smile and twisted her fingers together as he approached her. He put his arms around her. She stiffened in a way so unlike her normal cuddly self. Tentatively, she placed her hand on his back. Calum pressed his lips to her temple and held them there. 'Only sit with them if you want to. I won't be offended if you need space.'

'I'll be fine. You concentrate on the competition.'

'I'm not sure I can.' He kept his voice low. She tightened her grip, almost crushing him. 'I love you,' he whispered, so softly he wasn't sure if it had come out, but he couldn't hold it in any longer.

Rhona let out a whimper. Was it a cry or a laugh? Surely she wasn't laughing at that? 'Oh, Calum.'

'Just do what you have to.' He let her go, picked up his bags and gave them a wave as he trudged towards the competitors' entrance. His head was ringing. He'd told Rhona he loved her in front of his parents. He was sure they hadn't heard. Had Rhona? Her reaction had been odd but it didn't matter. He'd released some tension getting the words out. Now she knew. Now he knew. But knowing didn't make it any easier. If his parents' attitude over the last hour was anything to go by, things were about to get a whole lot worse.

Chapter Nineteen

Rhona

Rhona shivered. The sun beat down on the car park but she and Calum's parents were in the lee of the modern sports centre. It wasn't the shade cooling her blood. Calum had gone, leaving her with two people whose faces were serious and closed.

She adjusted her lightweight scarf and rubbed her arms. Before he left, Calum had whispered in her ear. *I love you. Holy shit!* He'd actually said it. Her stupid insides had transformed into jelly and she hadn't replied. Now he was gone.

'Oh god,' she said aloud. Why hadn't she said it back? She wanted him to know she loved him too. *So damn crazy much.* Could she go after him and tell him?

'Shall we go in?' Ron asked. 'Or would you prefer we left you alone?'

'I, er, I don't mind. I'm happy doing anything as long as I get to watch Calum.'

'Well, that's why we're all here,' Anne said. 'So let's put differences aside and support him.'

Rhona summoned a smile she hoped looked genuine. 'Sounds like a good plan.'

They joined a queue for the main door and Ron struck up a conversation with a stranger which excused Rhona from having to make small talk. Normally she could do that no bother but today it was like paddling against hostile waves.

If she and Calum were together, this would be what it was like. And worse. Once her family were in the mix too things would plummet. It wasn't like they could have big family birthday parties or Christmas dinners, not unless they wanted them to end with smashed crockery and broken hearts. She pushed her hair out of her face and sucked in a long slow breath.

Not wanting to rock the boat, she let Anne and Ron choose seats. They climbed the rattly steps on the giant pull-out stand in the arena. Rhona sat beside Anne, her arms tense and her entire body stiff.

'So, what is it you do?' Ron peered around his wife and smiled at Rhona. His bulky arms leaned on his knees. They were covered in tattoos, too many to take in but they seemed to have a nautical theme. She spotted ropes, anchors and a mermaid. It knocked her shell into a cocked hat.

'I'm an archaeologist.'

'Ah, that makes sense.' Ron exchanged a glance with Anne. 'Have you been working at Kilnarkie?'

'Yes.'

'Calum said he was having work done.'

'Did you find anything important?' Anne tucked a strand of burgundy hair behind her ear.

'Yes, I did. An Iron Age homestead; I found the hearth stone and parts of the outer wall.'

'So does that mean he can't build the house?' Anne's sharp and aquiline features were similar to Calum's. He'd taken most of his looks from her.

'He can once the report has been published. Everything's been mapped and recorded and I've made a reconstruction too so the history will be well documented.'

'Well, that's something,' Anne said. 'He paid a lot for that land; I wouldn't want it to be worthless.'

'It's a beautiful part of the island.' Ron rubbed his thick knees. 'He paid over and above to get it because he wanted to live there himself.'

'I don't think he ever will.' Anne side-eyed Rhona. 'There are too many complications.'

Yup. Rhona smiled, covering her inner sigh, and fiddled with her skirt. She scanned around, half hoping to spot someone she knew. If she did, she could jump ship and go talk to them. But a sea of unfamiliar faces swam before her.

Ron however seemed to know several people or spoke to them anyway. Rhona busied herself on her phone, checking up often and smiling their way so they wouldn't think her rude and ignorant. She messaged Cha and updated her. With her being far away, it was easier to confide. And for Rhona to hide her sense of gloom, framing it as an everyday nightmare occurrence in the life of Rhona Lamond.

CHA: Good god!!! Can you not escape? Go and sit somewhere else.

CHA: Stop the bus... rewind... You're seeing him? What about the thing with Arran? WTAF! He beat your brother to a pulp. Are you forgiving him? Did he give you a good reason? Because it better be bloody good. You don't want to see someone who might turn on you at any time.

Rhona flicked off the phone. That was still a mystery. She'd never discovered why Calum had hurt Arran. It seemed so unlikely that he would. But her parents were so insistent he'd done it in an unprovoked attack and Rhona had never questioned it. Until she'd met him. And then it didn't fit him at all. So much so, she hadn't even thought about it. The man she'd been with was so far from violent. Was it possible the whole thing was a mistake? Could Arran have lied? Maybe he fell but blamed it on Calum for whatever reason. Rhona winced. Was the whole family feud based on a lie?

The noise died down. An announcer walked out below and introduced the first round. The floor had been divided into four marked areas and eight competitors marched on together, splitting two to a mat. Rhona focused on Calum, red hot in his white karate suit, his black belt knotted around his waist.

All four matches would run simultaneously. That could get confusing. Rhona craned her neck and sat up straight, trying to keep Calum in her sightline. It was difficult as he was in a section not directly in front of them. Some spectators shuffled around. Rhona followed Ron and Anne as they ducked along the row for a better view.

Calum faced his opponent and bowed. For a few seconds they sparred and an adjudicator dressed in black hopped around watching closely. Rhona's heart rate increased. Calum kicked high and caught his opponent in the chest, knocking him to the ground. For someone so lean, he was strong. Ron jumped to his feet and punched the air. 'You get 'em, son.'

'Sit down,' Anne said, but she was laughing.

Rhona bit her lip. What was going on? Had he won? The adjudicator blew his whistle and pointed to Calum. Ron let out a roar of mirth. 'Yaas!'

Rhona smiled and clapped gently.

Calum and his opponent bowed, then shook. A lull followed as other matches played out. Rhona didn't need to fill the gaps, Ron was waxing lyrical on Calum's performance, explaining what moves he'd used. Whatever they were, Rhona just wanted to see him in action again.

She sat on her fingers, waiting. Once the first round was done, the areas were reset and the competitors marched on again. Calum's face was full of steely determination and Rhona's heart filled to the brim. He was her guy. She loved his determination. She loved that he'd succeeded in business. She loved that he was tough but cool under pressure. She loved his soft centre and how it came out for her. *I love him, full stop.* How could he have knowingly hurt her brother?

He squared up to his opponent and they sparred. 'Oh my god.' Rhona inhaled sharply as he narrowly blocked a punch, then almost knocked the feet from under his opponent. But not quite. This was a lot closer. She dug her nails into her cheeks and gasped as he ducked a kick.

'Come on,' Ron growled.

Calum's eyes seemed to blaze red and he unleashed a punch, kick combination that sent his opponent flying. Ron leapt to his feet again, roaring and shaking his fists with glee. 'That was bloody awesome.'

'Ron.' Anne slapped his leg. 'There are children in the crowd. Mind your language.'

'Wow.' Rhona slumped back, blowing out a sigh. 'That was nerve-racking.'

Anne turned to her and sucked in her lips. Rhona gave her a tentative smile. Could this be a moment of bonding?

'Don't you know about Calum and your brother?' Anne said.

'Well... yes.' The carpet came swooping out from under her feet, knocking her sideways faster than one of Calum's kicks could have done.

'I thought your parents would have told you all about it.' Anne's gaze was cool and her voice steady. 'That's why it surprises me that you want anything to do with him.'

Rhona blinked rapidly as she processed the words. They had told her. Of course they had. But discussing it here was the wrong time and place. Acid rose in her stomach, burning its way up her gut. Anne looked back at her son and Rhona followed suit, clapping as Calum left the arena. If she could focus on him and block out everything else, she could make this work. She had to.

Ron regurgitated the performance, beaming from ear to ear. Rhona jammed her hands under her armpits and restrained a shudder. What had made Calum attack Arran? She'd never asked him. She'd taken him at face value, as she'd done with Annike. Her parents' hatred of Calum must have some basis in fact. Had she let infatuation cloud her judgement? Or was she too afraid to hear the truth?

She gave herself a mental shake. What he'd done in the past didn't change the fact he'd always been gentle with her; he'd never shown any signs of violence. But what if he was unstable? She held her face, resting her elbows on her knees, and stared forward. A niggly ache prodded her tummy. *Find out the truth.* If she was going to enter into a relationship with him, she had a right to know exactly what had happened with him and Arran. But she wanted to hear it from him. Why had he never mentioned it before? Maybe for the same reason she'd never asked him. It didn't seem important when they were together. When she stepped back to view the bigger picture, she had to find out.

Anne looked too formidable to ask and she might spin the story if she thought it would scare Rhona away from her precious son. Rhona hated conflict. There was enough fighting below, they didn't need a verbal war in the stands.

'Quarter final next.' Ron rubbed his broad palms together.

The mats had been cleared and one centre stage set up. Rhona watched the first quarter, holding her breath and chewing her cuticles almost to bleeding point. These guys were fast and brutal. Could Calum match this kind of performance? She crossed her fingers.

When the first winner was announced, she clapped along, but her blood was thumping in her ears. Calum was up next. He strode out with a slightly shorter but much beefier guy. Rhona bit her lip. This was going to be tough. How could Calum make any inroads against that wall of muscle? Surely this guy would bludgeon him. She could hardly bear to watch. On the edge of her seat, she leaned forward as they bowed. The sparring was fast. The floor squeaked. Calum moved like lightning, ducking a punch, then throwing one of his own. It was a blur of suits, feet and fists. Ron growled and Anne gasped, clutching the chair. Rhona wasn't sure what was going on, but Calum avoided another punch and spin-kicked in such a way it caught his opponent square on the shoulder. From where he'd been seconds before it looked impossible.

'Bloody fantastic,' roared Ron. 'He has to get the win for that, he has to.'

The whistle blew and Calum and his opponent stepped back onto their coloured squares. The adjudicator retreated, blew his whistle again and pointed at Calum. Ron shook the whole row, jumping to his feet.

'No bloody way!' he yelled. 'He's in the semis. I don't believe it. This is bloody amazing!'

Rhona sat back in her seat and rubbed her sternum. *This is too much.* She needed air. Thankfully, only two more quarter-finals remained before they broke for lunch. She couldn't wait to get out, almost running down the stairs and joining the queue for the canteen. A few seconds later, she remembered to check for Anne and Ron. They were right behind her. What should she say? Before she could think of anything, she spotted Calum strolling towards them, dressed in joggers and a t-shirt. Rhona held back as Anne and Ron swamped him with praise and love.

'Thanks.' He untangled himself from their grip.

He'd miss that if they got together. Even if he'd lost in the first round, they would have greeted him with as much love and joy. They were so enraptured by him, it seemed possible even if he'd beaten up Arran for no reason they would have stood by him anyway. He was their boy.

Catching his eye, she smiled. He returned it, running his fingers through his damp hair.

'That was amazing.' She reached out and patted his arm. 'I don't know what's going on most of the time but it looked great.'

'I'm not sure what happened,' Calum said. 'I shouldn't really have beaten the last guy.'

'But you did,' Anne said.

'I did.' He stepped closer to Rhona and took her hand, squeezing it in his. 'You ok?'

She nodded. Her worries about what had happened with Arran all those years ago dispersed now Calum was back beside her. 'It's a bit nerve-racking.'

'Don't worry on my account. I've done better than I expected, so it's all good.'

'You should try it yourself,' Ron said. 'Karate's a great sport.'

'I have,' Rhona said. 'A bit. Calum practised some of his moves on me.'

'Did he now?' Ron pulled a giant grin, his eyebrows inching up his head.

'Oh my god.' Rhona clutched her cheeks. 'That came out all wrong.'

Ron burst out laughing and bent over holding his knees. Anne rolled her eyes.

'Seriously, Dad. It's not that funny.'

'Ron.' Anne's voice cracked like a whip. 'Stop being ridiculous.'

'That was friggin' hilarious,' he said. 'I'm so glad my son's moves don't disappoint.'

'She never said they didn't,' Calum muttered.

Rhona trod on his toe.

'Ow.'

She glanced up and winked. The ice thawed slightly after Ron's hysterics and with Calum back among them. Ron's jolly mood flowed into long stories and he kept them busy all through lunch accompanied by Anne's eye rolls. Rhona took the opportunity to focus on Calum, trying to telepathically extract the information about why he'd attacked Arran and also hoping to convey a reply to his words earlier. He flicked her a half smile. *But he doesn't have a clue what I'm thinking.* She'd have to wait until they were alone.

When they returned to the arena, they didn't have long to wait before the first semi-final. Calum came out with his eyes fixed forward, fists clenched at his sides.

Rhona didn't dare blink, the action was so fast. Calum got one kick in but his opponent was too fast and knocked him sideways with a punch. Rhona winced and Ron groaned. The adjudicator blew his whistle and pointed at the opponent. Rhona's shoulders sank, but Calum gave his opponent a smile as they shook. *Aw.* She interlaced her fingers and held them to her chest. He was proud of what he'd achieved and her heart swelled for him. He'd done so well. After the second semi, Calum came on again with the other losing semi-finalist.

'They play off for third place,' Ron answered Rhona's puzzled look.

'Oh.'

This time, Calum burst out fighting, he threw a kick and punch so fast the opponent bounced off.

'That's my boy,' Ron snarled. 'Go for it. Nothing to lose.'

But the opponent was another black belt who clearly knew what he was doing; he kicked back. Ron oohed and sucked in air with a whistle. Rhona kind of understood what Calum was doing. He couldn't knock this guy out, he was too skilled, but he was landing all the punches and kicks. The plan paid off. When the whistle blew, the adjudicator pointed at Calum and he exhaled visibly, closing his eyes with a grin and tossing back his head. When he opened them, he looked towards Rhona and winked.

She caught it like a lucky charm. *I love you.* She kissed her cupped fingers. Now, to get hold of the real man, tell him how she felt and get the truth from him.

Chapter Twenty

Calum

The bronze medal swung around Calum's neck and he straightened it on his chest. This was so far beyond what he'd dreamed of at the start of the day. He still wasn't sure how it had happened. Just knowing Rhona was watching had spurred him on to do his best.

'Right, guys, look this way.' A reporter aimed a camera at them.

Calum smiled so broadly he was sure no one would recognise him. His famous poker face was lost in this achievement. The gold and silver medal winners stood proud beside him. He patted their backs once the snaps were done. What would Will make of this? All the islanders in fact. Maybe his tenants would pay up on time if they discovered their landlord was a karate black belt and a bronze medallist too.

'Well done, guys,' he said.

'You too,' said the man with the gold, his semi-final conqueror. 'That was some play-off for third. Great kicks.'

'Thanks.' A proud bubble fizzed inside. Those three faces looking down on him and cheering him on meant the world. If only he could make them love each other as much as he loved them.

'Right, I need all your names,' the reporter said. 'And your clubs.'

Calum traced his finger over his medal, reading the words Argyll Karate Competition third place. This was like winning the lottery. The other two medallists had given their names.

'Calum Matheson. That's one *L* in Calum,' he said. 'And I'm not in a club.' Though maybe he should join one or start one of his own. Would anyone go? He was so unpopular on the island, he could see people boycotting it the second they saw his name. How much of that unpopularity had sprung from the Lamond's poisonous words?

Back in the locker room, he showered and changed into jeans and a smart t-shirt. Several guys patted him on the back and waved as they went their separate ways. Calum jostled through the crowd until he spied a shiny bald head, a burgundy hairdo and Rhona's long blonde hair. She turned and spotted him. The sight winded him harder than any of the punches he'd taken. That smile. She could undo him just by looking at him.

He reached her first, dropped his bags and fell into her waiting arms. Not caring who was watching, he bent in and kissed her on the temple. The scent of a warm rose garden engulfed him, blocking everything else. It was just the two of them. Everything was ok; how could it not be? What did it matter who her family were? Or if his parents liked her or not? He liked her and that was what mattered.

Rhona pulled away first, holding his gaze and bouncing like she was desperately trying to tell him something. Had his parents been awful to her? It wasn't in their nature to be unkind, but mention the Lamonds and it transformed them into terrors.

His eyes strayed to his mum. She stared back, arms folded. He blinked, not wanting to read anything into her look, but his brain had already started the analysis.

She didn't need to shake her head or open her mouth for him to know what she was thinking. *Don't be duped. You tried to be friends with a Lamond once before and look what happened.*

He released Rhona and pulled his parents into a group hug.

'You did it, son. You did it.' Ron wiped tears from his face. 'I couldn't be prouder.'

'Thanks, Dad.'

'Oh god, you'll make me cry too,' Anne said.

'What are you two like.' He turned back to Rhona and for the first time in a while he caught a glimpse of Arran in her. He'd almost forgotten what his former friend looked like, but something in her expression brought it back. He frowned and rubbed his chin. Arran had moved to the island at the beginning of secondary school, a tough time for anyone. He'd latched onto Calum. Calum wasn't a threat. Just a quiet, spotty boy who struggled to make friends. That was why Arran liked him. Calum rolled his shoulders. Arran was easily the more adventurous and naturally outgoing. Calum, not so much. When they were on their own, he was charming and they shared a lot of laughs but whenever Arran was in company he showed off, pretending Calum wasn't his friend and was just a joke. As soon as they were alone again, boom, he went back to normal, like nothing amiss had happened.

Arran hated Calum being better at anything or being first – the reason he'd asked out Hannah McDonald. Arran had no interest in her, until Calum said he liked her. Poor Hannah. She'd also been duped by Arran.

Rhona wasn't Arran and Calum had to remember that. If he trusted her now and kept on seeing her, she wouldn't shun him in public. He didn't want to keep up the pretence anymore. They'd had the last few weeks as a practice and today had been a trial but not a complete failure.

Since leaving school, Calum had done so much to prove he was as good as anyone. He'd made a success of his life. But had he served his sentence or got off scot-free?

If his parents were ok(ish) about this relationship, then Rhona's could be for her... But would they?

'Are we going for a meal?' Anne asked.

Rhona laced her fingers through Calum's and squeezed gently. He flicked her a quick glance and though she wasn't looking at him directly, he got her meaning. *Let's go home and celebrate together* – just the two of them. He didn't blame her. It couldn't have been an easy day. A night alone together would be a relaxing end to a stressful day.

'Let's go home,' Calum said. 'I'm exhausted after that.'

'No wonder. Bronze medallist, eh.' Ron fake-punched him. 'Here you were expecting to be out in round one and now look at you.'

They headed back to the car, Ron still replaying the day.

'This'll keep him going in the pub for several weeks,' Calum whispered in Rhona's ear. 'He loves bragging to his mates.'

'He's proud of you,' she said. 'And so am I.'

He put his arm around her. 'Let's get to the ferry.'

The hulking black and white ship was on its way in as Calum drove into the lane and pulled on the handbrake. He peeped sideways at Rhona and they exchanged another smile, Ron still yapping in the back seat. He didn't stop as Calum steered onto the boat and even as they got out and shut the doors, he carried on.

Anne rolled her eyes as they made their way to the stairs. 'This is why I still work. Otherwise, I'd go deaf or die of boredom.'

Rhona giggled and Calum's shoulders loosened. The thaw was still happening. Slowly but surely.

'Who's for a drink?' Ron said as soon as they got to the upper deck.

'Sorry, Dad, I need some air,' Calum said. 'It was so stuffy in the sports centre.'

'Me too,' Rhona said.

'Ok, off you go,' Ron said. 'I'm going to the bar.'

'I could murder a gin.' Anne followed him.

Calum nudged open the door and claimed the fresh air; it filled his chest with hope. 'Sorry about my dad, he talks far too much.'

'He's funny.'

'So... Does that mean you don't hate him?' Calum took her hand and they strolled towards the back of the boat.

'I don't,' she said. 'But it wasn't the easiest afternoon. It was hard work.'

Calum looped his arms around her waist. 'I'm sorry you had to go through it alone.' Should he ask her if she'd heard what he said earlier? Or say it again? 'I'd like this to be ok... for us at least to try.'

'I think your parents will come round before mine. Your mum and dad love you so much, they want you to be happy.' She reached up and traced her finger around his neck. 'My parents... Well, you saw what they were like after the boat trip. They're overprotective and rigid about hating you.'

Calum ran his thumb down her cheek. 'I wish it wasn't so complicated.' Her wide eyes bored into his. He dipped in and kissed her, tasting her strawberry lips. She melted into him and he forgot where they were. He gathered her closer, kissing her full on until he couldn't breathe.

'I can't wait to get home,' Rhona whispered.

'Me neither.' Gently, he steered her around, then stood behind her enveloping her in a hug. Quietly, they watched the view as the wind whistled by. Every so often Calum bent in and kissed her. The great fortress of Duart Castle came into view. They were nearing Mull.

'You know what I said earlier,' Calum murmured in her ear. He wanted to say it again but first, he had to discover her feelings. She hadn't said anything and even in the time they'd been here, she hadn't spoken. His heart pounded. What if she wasn't ready for this? Had he pushed her too fast? Maybe deep down she still didn't trust him. Hell, he'd never explained why he'd beaten up her brother at school and his excuse was bordering on threadbare. She had every right not to want him in the long run. Why was he thinking about inflicting himself on her? After being careful for so long, he'd let himself go. Wasn't protecting the woman he loved more important than having her?

'I heard and, well... I need to ask you something.' He stepped back, releasing her, and leaned on the railing. Her eyes dulled and he was sure he wasn't going to like it. He was wedged in the corner, quite literally, trapped. His pulse drummed in his ears. On one side, the walkway ran down the ship's port side. Behind Rhona, the path crossed the ship, meeting a large staircase to the upper viewing deck. Over her shoulder, he spotted his parents coming around the corner on the far side. *Shit.* Their timing was bloody terrible.

'Not now.' He rubbed his chin, dropping his gaze. 'I want to hear whatever it is but let's wait until we're alone.' As he lifted his head to the side walkway, he did a double take. Blinking, his mouth fell open. A man had come out on deck. He crossed the walkway and leaned his forearms on the railings. The wind ruffled the tufts of blond hair at his forehead as he stared out to sea. The hairs on Calum's neck raised and he ground his teeth. *Surely not?*

Perhaps aware of Calum's stare, the man looked around. Calum stood tall, his jaw stiffening, fists balling at his sides. The man straightened up too and narrowed his eyes. A rush of anger burst through Calum, his pulse hammering in his ears.

'Arran! What are you doing here?' Rhona's voice called out but it seemed far away.

Before Calum could say another word, she ran to him and threw her arms around her big brother. *What? No!* Calum gaped. Blood rushed from his head, clogging his limbs and numbing his entire body. His chest imploded and he staggered back, colliding with the railing.

Chapter Twenty-One

Rhona

Rhona fixed her arms around Arran's neck. He was tugging to get away but clinging on might divert his attention away from Calum.

'Rhona! Let me go, will you?' Arran laughed, wrenching himself free and rolling his shoulders. 'Are you trying to throttle me? I know you miss me but seriously.'

Tentatively, Rhona edged back, her focus travelling to where Calum was still standing in the corner. His fist gripped the neck of his shirt. Rhona's heart throbbed, seeing him alone. Abandoned and forgotten. She was ready for her family to find out about their relationship, but not like this. Arran would flip. Breaking it gently and gradually was the key and she needed to be clear first. Calum's story was important. Hearing it from him and not second-hand was vital. Who else could she trust to tell the whole truth?

'What are you doing here?' She thrust her hands into her back pockets and dragged her gaze away from Calum. 'I thought you weren't coming until tomorrow?'

'I got here quicker than I expected. It'll be fun to surprise Mum and Dad. Mum gets so stressed when she's waiting for me. This way she won't have to worry.' Arran rubbed his fist in his palm and screwed up his face, looking over Rhona's shoulder.

Shit. It was blatantly obvious who he was glowering at. Blinking, Rhona followed his sightline. 'Oh, that's eh... Calum, isn't it?' Heat stung her cheeks. Calum ran his fingers around his chin, then turned away to where his parents were approaching from the other direction.

'Yeah.' Arran's jaw set. 'Calum bloody Matheson.' He grabbed Rhona's arm, leading her in the opposite direction. 'So, have you been shopping or something?'

'What? Oh...' What the hell was she supposed to do now? Confessing to Arran wasn't an option but she couldn't abandon Calum.

She glanced back at him. He frowned and shook his head.

I'm coming back, wait. Just wait. I need to divert Arran first. Focusing with all her might, she tried to impart the message to him telepathically. Anne and Ron appeared at his side. Anne pursed her lips, looking ready to spit on the ground. She rested her hand on Calum's back and they stalked out of sight.

Rhona's ears rang as her heart walloped. *No, no, no. Wait. Please wait.* Who should she go to? What should she do?

'Rhona?' Arran gaped at her. 'Are you listening?'

'What?'

'Have you been shopping?'

'Oh, er, yes.' She swallowed.

'What are you looking at? Was Calum Matheson giving you trouble before I came out?'

'No, nothing like that.'

'I hate that dick.' He put his arm around Rhona's shoulder, tugging her away from the Mathesons.

'He's not that bad,' Rhona said. 'I, em, I've been working for him, and he's ok.'

'Working for him? Have you lost your mind?' Arran's arm dropped to his side and he balled his fists.

'No. It was an interesting project.'

'Was? Does that mean you're finished?'

She nodded.

'Thank Christ. Keep away from him in the future. You've no idea what he's like. He's a brute.'

'He was very polite to me,' she said. What a ridiculous cop-out.

'Oh yeah? Turned on the charm for you, did he? Well, watch him. He's totally unstable. One minute he's your best friend, the next he's smashing you to a pulp, and if he lays a finger on my little sister, I'll make sure he's banged up and never sees the light of day again.'

Rhona managed a weak smile. She appreciated Arran's concern but the idea of Calum doing anything like that to her was incomprehensible. He just wouldn't. She'd made mistakes of the heart; she'd trusted people when they turned out to be work-stealing bitches, but this time, she was sure.

'What actually happened?' she said.

'Don't you remember? He turned on me and I didn't have a chance to defend myself. He's a psycho. Remember my face? It was purple and swollen for weeks.'

How could she forget? If he'd done it once did that mean there was a chance he could do it again? Was that the reason for the karate and his avoidance of intimacy and relationships? Did he fear himself? Had he found a safe outlet for his anger?

The twinge in her stomach was back. She felt sick. What a mess. Where did this leave them? Calum had let her in and that had to count for something... But what? Love? Could love stop him attacking again if the same mad demons seized him? Unprovoked demons?

As Arran chatted, she pulled out her phone. Her fingers trembled as she typed in a message, angling the screen away from him. If he saw the name... She didn't want to think about what he might do.

RHONA: Sorry, I better go with Arran. I wanted to divert him. Talk soon. I hope we're still ok. XXX

And she meant it. If everything could just be ok; the way it had been for the last couple of months.

With Arran back home that seemed next to impossible.

'Why do you stick with archaeology?' Arran said. 'If you end up working for knobs like him. I've got loads of good contacts these days and I could get you into something much more lucrative. You wouldn't need to retrain or anything. It's all stuff you can pick up as you go along.'

Seriously? Rhona couldn't muster the energy to reply.

Judy exploded with excitement when Rhona and Arran came in together.

'What a surprise! Oh my goodness. I need to message Alister to come back. Rhona, could you do it? Tell him to come home straightaway. In fact, tell him to pick up some smoked salmon on the way home.' She seized Arran and wrestled him into a huge hug. 'Oh, son, it's so good to see you. If only we could get your big sisters here too. I miss having us all together.'

Rhona lifted an eyebrow. The last time they'd all been together her sisters had fallen out withing seconds of seeing each other and she'd spent the weekend trying to get them talking again. She took out her phone and slumped onto a sofa while her mum fawned over Arran on the one opposite. Her head throbbed and her heart wept. She hashed out a message to her dad, then refreshed the screen several times, desperate for any word from Calum.

Did I make the right decision? What would have happened if she'd gone with him? Would he and Arran have had a punch-up on the ferry? If they'd faced off, Rhona would put money on Arran being the one to strike first. Arran could be hot-headed and Calum was more likely to have mastery of himself, but if he fought back, Arran would come off worse, if today's display was anything to go by. *You've been wrong about people before!* A vision of Annike's smug face swam before her. That was her biggest misjudgement so far. Could Calum turn out to be even more of a gargantuan mistake? She tapped the sofa arm and looked into the garden. Branches swayed around the tree house. When they'd kissed in there, the buzz had been incredible. *So what? Am I just infatuated?* Had it stopped her from seeing reason? Could she not see the wood for the trees?

'Did you have a good day?' Judy asked.

'Yes.' Rhona summoned her best smile.

'Did you buy anything?'

'No, just browsed.'

'Who were you with again?'

'Oh... Just me.'

'You'll never guess who was on the boat.' Arran's expression darkened. Couldn't he let go? Smile and lighten up? He was a good-looking guy but that face made him so bitter.

'Who?'

'Bloody Calum Matheson.'

'Oh no.' Judy tapped her foot on the lino. 'I love living here but those Mathesons make life so difficult. I wish they'd move away.'

'Yeah, and he was harassing Rhona by the looks of things, wasn't he?'

'No, he wasn't,' Rhona said. 'I told you.'

'I saw the way he was looking at you. If he hadn't said anything, he was about to.'

'What is going on with you and him?' Judy asked. 'After that boat fiasco. I'd never have forgiven him if anything had happened to you. I hope he's not got some hold on you. You have to tell us if he does.'

'Seriously, Mum.' Rhona slapped her fingertips to her forehead. 'Nothing happened on the boat.' Nothing bad anyway. Just one amazing night.

'I'll stop when I'm sure he can do no more damage and that'll be the day he either leaves this island or gets locked up.'

'What boat are we talking about?' Arran said.

'Rhona went off on his boat with him to Coll.' Judy pursed her lips and narrowed her eyes. 'And I'm still very dubious about his motives.'

'What the hell?' Arran gaped at Judy, then turned to Rhona. 'I will fucking kill him.'

Her chest burned with the constant vitriol they threw at Calum. Telling the truth was what she wanted to do but that would backfire like a misloaded cannon and cause even more pain.

'Apparently it was an archaeology trip,' Judy said before Rhona opened her mouth. 'The idiot hadn't checked the weather forecast and, what do you know, a storm blew in and they were stranded overnight. We got a message from the coastguard. I nearly died of shock. Didn't sleep a wink for worrying.'

'It wasn't like that,' Rhona said. 'He had checked the forecast but weather changes all the time out here.'

'Jesus Christ, if I'd known that, I'd have given him what for,' Arran said. 'Was it just you and him?'

Rhona nodded, barely restraining her eye roll.

'You went to Coll alone on a boat with him?' Arran glared at her. 'Have you completely lost the plot? Or did he force you? He better not have.'

'He didn't force me to do anything. He's an ok guy really.' Her voice was weak, barely more than a whimper. This conversation was draining. The entire situation leached the life from her. Why did they go on and on like this? Round and round, rehashing the same old arguments, refusing to see any possible changes. 'All this stuff you say about him being violent, I've never seen it.' *Unless you include today.* She'd spent hours watching him fight. But that was different. Very different, right?

'Not yet. Give him time,' Arran said. 'He's good at bottling it. He's like the picture of calm, then one day he snaps.'

'It's true,' Judy said. 'He has a terrible temper. Only last year, it was all around the island how he was trying to evict tenants by forcing up their rents and threatening them. He's a bully.'

Rhona massaged her temples. She wanted the truth. Calum's version of the truth. But years of not trusting Matheson's had been drilled into her and the simplest thing to do was to let him go. She would find someone else given time, wouldn't she? Tears threatened and her throat burned. She fought to keep her face neutral and calm. *How can I even think that? I don't want anyone else.* She wanted Calum. She loved him. But having him was a different matter. Someone was going to get hurt and if she wasn't the one to crush him, however unintentionally, her family would do it for her.

Chapter Twenty-Two

Calum

The words from Rhona's text were imprinted on the inside of Calum's brain. Ron and Anne had done everything to 'console' him. Or so they thought. And maybe he should praise their efforts. If he'd broken up with Rhona, he could count on them to be there full of commiseration along with a big dollop of shit to slap on the faces of those dreadful Lamonds.

He sat in his flat, massaging his temples. A few hours ago he'd been on cloud nine; he'd come third in a karate competition and told Rhona he loved her. Now he was here alone. He'd watched her walk off with Arran. Was that how it would always be? Lovers in secret, as long as no one knew.

Apathy descended on him and he slouched on his leather couch, staring over the marina, flipping his phone. Should he reply? Say what? He'd told her exactly how he felt that morning. Words he'd never said to anyone except his mum and dad. She hadn't said anything in return. The noise she'd made had sounded like a laugh. Why would she laugh about that? Maybe love was several steps too far for her. She wanted to keep seeing him while she was here, while it was convenient, but not forever. She showered him with affection but it wasn't the same as love. Rhona threw affection around freely. Was he a fool to think he was special?

His phone flashed and another message lit the screen.

RHONA: Please don't give me the silent treatment. I'm so confused and I'm not sure what to do. Are we still ok? I guess while Arran's on the island, it's not a good idea for us to see each other. I wanted to ask you what happened when you were at school. Why did you do it? Sorry, I just need to know. I miss you already XXX

Chewing the inside of his lip, he opened a reply box.

CALUM: I'm not giving you the silent treatment. I'm giving you the space you need. I'm sure Arran's told you the story. Take care. X

It was a copout, a total copout. The impersonal shit he did so well. Robot Calum was back. He could get up tomorrow, go to his office and work. Sunday was as good a day as any. Shutting down was easier than facing up to what had happened. Arran's arrival gave him a cast-iron excuse to stay away. His side of the story didn't matter. The bottom line was, he'd done it. Nothing could excuse it. He'd unleashed a violent attack on a classmate. End of.

With no shortage of jobs to do, he could occupy himself all week. The only thing he had to be around for was Beth's wedding on Friday. Something he could do without. He wasn't in the mood for a party, but if he attended the service, he could pay his respects and skip the evening do without feeling too guilty. She'd been a friend since their school days but they weren't bosom buddies. If he wasn't sitting on a pew come her big day, would she even notice? Would anyone? Some people might even be relieved by his absence.

He laid out his dress kilt on Thursday evening, gritting his teeth and forcing himself not to think of Rhona, but she kept popping into his brain. How much more fun would this be if she was on his arm? Infinitely. Well, she wouldn't be there, though Arran would. Could he avoid another face-off?

He grabbed his phone and called Will.

'Hey,' Will said. 'What's up?'

'Arran Lamond is back.'

'Yeah, I heard that.'

'I assume he'll be at the wedding tomorrow.' Calum paced, keeping the phone glued to his ear.

'I think so. I met Frank.'

Frank was Beth's best pal and the opposite of Arran. Frank always smiled, laughed and made mischief – the fun kind. At school, his antics had annoyed Calum but now... Well, maybe he'd had the best solution: laugh everything off, then leave the island at the first opportunity.

'And?'

'He said Arran had come back this week so he could attend. Frank wasn't best pleased. Arran was always a bit mean to him at school, though you know Frank, he never takes anything too seriously.'

'A bit mean? Christ, that's like calling Satan naughty.' The security of having his dad as a teacher in the same school had made Arran think he was invincible, until Calum had snapped.

'Yeah,' Will said.

Why was Will so accepting? How could anyone think what Arran had done was forgivable? He'd picked on Calum for his spots, Frank for being gay, Beth for being a tomboy, Will for not being sporty and Hannah MacDonald for being chubby – though it hadn't stopped him snogging her to get one over on Calum – and they weren't the only ones. But somehow, he'd stayed popular and unchallenged. Almost. Until that fateful day.

'I wish I never had to see him again.'

'Stick with us,' Will said. 'And it'll be fine.'

Yeah. Just fine. Would anything ever be just fine ever again?

Calum arrived early at the church and sat in his 4X4 watching the trees swaying in front of the compact and pleasing-to-the-eye building. It had that typical austere island style but a haunting charm hung about it with the rolling hills behind and the sea out front. Cars pulled up, lining the road on either side and Calum kept his head down, pretending to browse his phone, while peeking up to see if Arran had arrived yet... Or Will. Where was Will? Once he was here it would be safe to get out.

Familiar faces passed by dressed in their kilts, suits or best dresses. Most of the women were holding onto their fascinators or adjusting their hair as the wind picked up from the sea. Apart from a few strong gusts however it was a beautiful day.

Robyn and Carl Hansen, two former classmates who'd married the year before, arrived. Robyn was another one Arran had mocked for her shocking crime of being too intelligent. Donald and Ida Laird, Will's parents, followed up the path. Still no Will. Then came Georgia Rose, a young local artist, dressed like a nineteen-fifties film star on the arm of her new husband, local landowner Archie Crichton-Leith. If Will didn't show, Calum would be safe with those two. They were heavily involved in Rebekah's affordable housing project and Calum could talk business with them for hours.

He raised his eyebrow as he watched them amble up the path. Like they'd want to talk shop? They looked totally loved-up. He glanced back at his phone before checking up again. *Oh god*. Arran was strutting up the road and he wasn't alone. Rhona was with him. *Shit*. Why?

She was friends with Beth's sister and had probably come along to support her... it made sense, but Christ, he'd ignored her for a week, shoved her out of his mind, denied himself every thought about her. She must have known he'd be there. She had to. Was she there to see him? Her pink satin dress clung to her curves and swung off her hips, fluttering around her knees. Stunning. Her hair was pinned loosely back with elegant curls escaping at the front but her head was bowed and her expression deflated. Not at all like the Rhona he was used to. His heart frosted over. *It's my doing.* He'd hurt her. Not physically, but emotionally. She'd chosen to go with Arran on the boat and he couldn't deal with it. Even now it made him sick. He didn't blame her for choosing her family over him but he didn't like it either.

A banging on his window startled him. 'Jesus, Will. You gave me a heart attack.'

Will beamed in and waved. Calum jumped out. Beside Will, Morven smiled, stroking a pristine white bib down Angus's front, covering a cute little sailor suit.

'All looking good,' Calum said. Will's kilt seemed to bounce as he headed through the gate and Morven's floral dress swayed.

A large green tractor was parked in front of the church with ribbons on the front tied in a huge bow.

'Typical Beth.' Will chortled.

'Is she going to drive them away in that?' Calum said.

'She certainly is. I do love her. She's so funny.'

'God knows what the groom makes of it,' Morven said.

'Murray loves it,' Will said. 'They make such a great couple. I remember when they first met – they hated each other, but it turned out well.'

'Listen,' Calum said. 'Arran's inside already and I don't want to talk to him or go anywhere near him, ok?' He glared at Will.

'I'm not that fussed to either. He's not exactly my greatest pal.'

'Good.' They'd cleared that up. Will was all for building bridges normally but the thought of seeing Arran again would have rattled him.

'We should sit near the back anyway,' Morven said. 'In case Angus starts screaming and we need to get him out.'

Half the back row was free and Calum let Will and Morven take their seats before he perched at the end of a pew. Within seconds his gaze zeroed in on Rhona and Arran. The murmur of voices grew fuzzy. Will was talking about Murray, the groom, who was at the front, adjusting his cuffs and looking uber smart in a modern charcoal kilt suit. Calum had skimmed him over, barely distinguishing one word of what Will was saying. Every atom in his body was concentrated on Rhona. The force of desire rushing through him was so powerful he half expected the stained-glass windows to shatter or the altar candles to erupt in shooting flames.

Rhona's head slowly turned as he knew it would. Like he was commanding her. Their gazes connected and her brows raised. The sparkle in her irises had dulled and she wore a sorrowful expression. Only last week he'd said three precious little words to her. Three words he'd meant with body and soul and she'd barely acknowledged them.

The gentle organ music that had been playing in the background stopped. Its absence left an eerie hush, broken only by shuffling feet and low mumbles.

'Please rise,' the minister said.

Rhona faced forward again and Calum got to his feet.

At the front, the groom stood tall, hands clasped in front of him and the music started again, louder and prouder. This was the kind of thing Ron and Anne dreamed of for Calum. And with Rhona the tiniest whisper of possibility had edged its way in. In his heart anyway. But now?

The back doors opened and heads turned. Calum forced himself to look too, though his eyes demanded to see Rhona again. *Stay focused.* Beth stepped onto the carpeted aisle, her svelte figure encased in a plain but elegant sheath dress. Her dark hair was knotted in a low bun. Even in his messed-up state, Calum let out a breath of appreciation. Beth had always been a farmer, more used to wearing overalls and mucky jeans, but now she was like something straight off the catwalk. Her long slender arm was looped around her mother's. Calum's throat burned. He swallowed, remembering Beth had lost her dad some years ago and reminding himself how lucky he was to still have both his parents. Behind them walked her sister in a short pink dress, matching their mother's suit, and Frank in a grey kilt and pink shirt. He wiped away a tear as he passed and flicked his tufty blond fringe.

'Ahh,' Will whispered. 'She's so beautiful.'

As they sat, Calum's phone vibrated in his sporran. *Seriously?* Not an appropriate time or place. How could he get it out and switch it off without everyone tutting and muttering? *Typical Matheson, always on his phone, cutting another penny-pinching deal.* He'd heard it all before. Even if he didn't feel he belonged to the reputation, he had it anyway. Attempting to get the phone out quietly was like opening a bag of sweets in the cinema without rustling it.

Will squinted at him curiously and Calum pretended not to notice, staring forward. The minister's words washed over him. Without looking down, he fumbled around and pulled out his phone, sliding it onto the seat beside him. He glimpsed the screen and noted straightaway a message from Rhona.

His face woke the phone and he lowered his eyes, trying to read the message without it being too obvious.

RHONA: We need to talk. What's going on? This was always going to be tough when it hit. Now we're in the eye of the storm and every course is scary. I hope I didn't hurt you going off with Arran on the boat. I had to. I still want to hear your side of the story. It's important. I'll try to get away from him today, and maybe we could chat after? XX

He shook his head at the screen. *Hurt me? By walking off with my nemesis and leaving me alone to stew? Why would that hurt me?* He'd laid his feelings on the line and she'd chosen to ignore them. No, not ignore them, dismiss them.

None of it could make him innocent because he wasn't.

Maybe it was better like this. He didn't want to do the clandestine thing. How could he? It was mockery, like his feelings weren't valid and had to be hidden away to appease a family that had made his life a misery for years. *No.*

He should have known she'd do something like this. Once a Lamond, always a Lamond.

She was a talented archaeologist. If she got a call to dig up the lost treasure of the Aztecs next week, she'd be off in a flash. He'd been a fool to believe otherwise. Definitely better this way.

'Excuse me.' He jumped off the pew, nipped out the back door and stood on the step, breathing the fresh air. He couldn't stand another second of this.

His fingers flashed across the screen.

CALUM: I can't do this. My hand was forced last weekend when my parents decided to come with me to the karate competition. It wasn't easy but we got through it. Maybe meeting Arran on the boat wasn't the time or place for us to come clean, but instead of facing it head-on, you chose to go with him. Even now, you won't speak to me when he's there. I was ready to give it a go and I thought you were too, but with hindsight you've made the right choice. My behaviour at school was inexcusable. I hurt Arran and I shouldn't have. Ever since I got close to you, I've worried that somewhere down the line that monster will show up in me again. I can't risk it. Let's stop this while we can.

He reread it but no matter what he said, it didn't do justice to his heart. What he craved was to go back inside, crowd-surf to her, pluck her out, hold her in his arms, and tell her he'd love her forever. But no. Arran would murder them both. Even if he restrained himself, Rhona's family would make sure he died a long painful death. Christ, they would probably disown her if she confessed to love him in return, and she wouldn't want that.

'And, fuck, neither do I.' He marched to his car without a backward glance. *Leave her. Leave her alone. It's the only way.* As long as he was in her life, he'd ruin it.

Chapter Twenty-Three

Rhona

Rhona dabbed at her tears. Crying at a wedding was perfectly acceptable. The newly-weds wrestled their way into the tractor causing enough of a distraction for Rhona to disappear into her own thoughts. She half laughed in spite of herself as Murray held Beth's posy and she settled into the driver's seat.

'She always was a firecracker,' Arran said.

'Yeah,' Rhona agreed. Some people were brave. Brave enough to have a crazy wedding where they left in a tractor. Brave enough to follow their hearts. *And then there are people like me.* People who let the world pass them by, avoiding confrontation. She'd scanned the crowd constantly and not seen sight or sound of Calum. Will and Morven were standing nearby, beaming and waving as the tractor rumbled down the path to the gate. Nope, Calum definitely wasn't here. But his message would never leave.

The truth hurt and Rhona couldn't bear to read it a second time. Maybe he was right. She didn't want to be with someone violent but it all felt wrong.

Arran had swaggered off and was talking to a group of women. Rhona frowned. The way his chest was thrown out and his lips curled into a smug grin made him look like the lad about town. He'd had an on-off relationship with a woman for several years. Presumably it was in an off phase. Rhona didn't ask too many questions but something about his bluster gave her a discontented prickle. This was the arrogant side to Arran she tried to ignore but sometimes it was hard. Her sisters had it too. Maybe even her mum. A selfishness she ignored because they were her family.

She caught Will's eye and he smiled before his gaze travelled over Arran. Was it her imagination or did he look nervous? Why? Weren't they old school friends? Or had Will picked the Matheson camp?

'Back in a minute,' Arran said to the women in a carrying voice. His eyes narrowed at Will who turned away and put his arm around Morven.

'I forgot about Silly Willy,' he said. 'Thank Christ his bum chum didn't come along too.'

Rhona didn't reply. What was the point? She daren't let on that Calum had been here.

'I still can't believe you took on a job for him,' Arran muttered.

'Well, there's not a lot of work here.' The words pierced her chest. She'd held back applying for anything while she was working for Calum but now that work was finished and their future was ropey, she had to start searching again.

'Then get the fuck back to Europe,' Arran said. 'Don't hang around here. I can see Calum coming up with lots more "work" for you, then paying you shit or discrediting you.'

Rhona clamped her lips shut, biting down the things she'd love to say if she dared.

'Now, listen. Where are your friends?'

'Kirsten's with the bridal party.'

'You stick with her for a bit. I'm going to chat with these ladies again and I'm not sure I need you hanging around, little sis. Kinda cramps my style.'

'How will you get there if I don't drive you?'

'I'll cadge a lift with these ladies.'

'Ok. Fine. I'll see you later.'

'Thanks.' He cuffed her upper arm.

Best excuse ever. She jumped into the car and drove towards Tobermory. No one would miss her for a bit. The evening party didn't officially start for a few hours yet and she had to find Calum. She wasn't risking another message, this had to happen face to face.

But he wasn't at home or in his office. Or he wasn't answering if he was.

No luck. She returned to the wedding party. And what for? To hang about drinking soda water all evening so she could be Arran's taxi? She whiled away the hours inside the barn, watching the dancing unfold under the fairy lights, sharing a few laughs with random people and snatching the odd chat with Kirsten.

'Hey.' A woman with a blonde tousled bob sat beside her. 'How are you?'

It took her a few seconds to scramble her mind together and remember who the woman was. 'Hi, Georgia.' She was a friend of Kirsten's Rhona had met on a visit a couple of years before. 'I'm ok. You?'

'All good,' she said. 'This is so cute, isn't it? Beth's the biggest closet romantic on the island.'

'I thought that was you,' Rhona said.

'I'm not in the closet about it.' She grinned and took a sip from a tall glass.

Rhona tried to laugh along. She remembered Georgia being chatty and fun but nothing could pull her out of this mood.

'Is that your brother?' Georgia indicated Arran who was downing shots at the bar and laughing far too loudly.

'Yup. I should take him home. He looks wasted.'

'Probably a good idea.'

Getting Arran in the car was a struggle, driving home, worse. Rhona had to stop several times for him to keel over in the verge and throw up. But it was better that than returning home with sick stains on the upholstery. Mum would have a fit.

'Please, Arran. Get back in and try to hold it in. I'm exhausted.'

He barely made it in the door before he launched himself into the downstairs bathroom. Rhona left him to it and went to bed.

Judy spent the following morning panicking about Arran. 'I think he's ill. Did he eat something funny last night?'

Rhona couldn't help rolling her eyes. What a sad man he was. Thirty-three and still behaving like he was ten years younger. He didn't show face until the afternoon. The pallor of his skin when he finally emerged reinforced Judy's insistence that he must be ill. She laid her palm on his forehead.

'Mum,' he groaned. 'I'm fine. I just need air.'

Rhona sucked in her lip, taking pity on him as Judy fussed around. 'I'll go for a walk with you if you like.'

'Yeah, let's go.' He scraped back his chair.

Rhona's feet led her in the same direction she'd walked over the past few weeks. At the gate to the track running to Kilnarkie was a maroon people carrier that was vaguely familiar. A friend of her dad's maybe but definitely not Calum's 4x4. That brought a wash of relief.

The pull of the dig site was strong. She wanted to show Arran exactly what she did. The opportunity hadn't come up. He dissed her job like it was worthless, she could show him her office – who wouldn't be impressed by the wide-open beauty of Kilnarkie?

'See over there.' She pointed towards the greensward sloping to a white sandy beach and the sea beyond. 'That's where I was working.'

'Are you messing with me? Is this Matheson's land?'

'The part down here is. Come and see. I'll show you the dig.'

'What the hell for?' Arran screwed up his face. 'What if he's there?'

'He won't be.' Her stomach squirmed. He wouldn't come out here on a Saturday. Would he?

'Fine, let's do it. I can't believe he owns this land now. We used to play here. What's he going to do with it? Build the Berlin Wall and make sure no one can enjoy it except himself.'

'His house plans looked gorgeous and environmentally sensitive. This would be a beautiful place to live.' As it had been once for an Iron Age family and she'd preserved their humble home in a reconstruction.

'Well, let's see what his illicit cash buys him.'

'Why is it illicit?'

'It must be,' Arran said. 'You know where he grew up. There's no way he made that money legitimately'

'Why not?'

'Everyone says it. It's not just me.'

'Sounds like everyone's jealous.'

'Ha. Jealous of that dick. I don't think so. You tell me how he did it then? What did he tell you?'

'He inherited a property.' Her heart shrank a little more. What if he had done something else illegally? Was inheriting one property enough to start all this? She'd accepted what he'd told her. Was that her being too trusting again? Should she have demanded to know exactly how he'd built his business? Did people do that? Vet potential partners for criminal tendencies?

A few tattered clouds blew across the sky as they strolled towards the fences surrounding the dig. Rhona was convinced Calum wouldn't be there, but she let out a sigh of relief that no cars were in the quarry car park at the site edge.

She led Arran through the barrier. 'This is my trench, over here. Come on. It's not that mucky. I can show you the reconstruction when we get back but if you look over here first you can see the hearth.'

'The what? I don't get why you find this stuff interesting.' He shoved his hands in his pockets. 'It's just soil.'

Rhona smacked her forehead. Even Calum wasn't this bad, latterly he'd attempted to take an interest.

'How does he afford this? He must have ripped someone off somewhere. Loads of people in fact. I heard he's been raising rents all around the island and being a right bastard. One of these days...' Arran rammed his fist into his palm. 'He'll get what's coming to him.'

'Will I?'

Rhona leapt about two feet before spinning around. Calum stood atop the trench, Will Laird beside him with his baby strapped to his front. He grabbed Calum's arm, but a red light glinted in Calum's eye. The same expression he'd sported when staring down opponents at the karate competition.

His chest rose and fell slowly. 'You always thought you were really someone. And now you can't stand that I have all this.'

'Fuck off.' Arran snorted.

'Don't you dare speak like that in front of a child.'

'Arran, please.' Rhona grabbed his arm but he shrugged her off.

'Get off me.'

'You wouldn't recognise success if it slapped you,' Calum said.

'How would you know?' Arran said. 'At least what I earn is legit, unlike you.'

'Every penny I've ever made is as legit as you. You only wish it wasn't because it makes you look pathetic.'

'Come on, Rhona. We're done here.' Arran jumped out of the trench and glared at Calum. They were similar in height and both towering in their rage. Was this the monster he'd warned her about? She couldn't bear to see it. 'And that's the last dealings you'll be having with my sister. She won't be working for you anymore.'

'Working for me?' Calum stared at her.

'Arran, pipe down.' Rhona scrambled out of the ditch.

'Hey,' Will said. 'Why don't we take a breather.'

'I mean it.' Arran glared at Calum. 'Never again. She's not working for you and you can keep your sleezy hands off her.'

'Arran,' Rhona snapped.

'I beg your pardon?' Calum clenched his fists and his nostrils flared. 'Is that what I've been doing?' He glowered at Rhona.

She shook her head, her eyes wide. Of course it wasn't. She opened her mouth—

'Just leave, both of you. I shouldn't have expected anything less from you.' He eyeballed Rhona. 'You're just like the rest of them.'

'But, Calum.' Her heart split like he'd rammed in a knife. *I'm not.* She wanted to protect him from what her family might do to him but the cost was agonising.

'But what?' Calum's cool was visibly slipping. 'Are you going to tell him the truth?'

Arran glared between Calum and Rhona while Rhona mouthed air, but no words came out. Will took hold of Calum's arm again but Calum pulled away.

'No, of course you're not. Get off my land. Both of you. And don't bother coming back.'

'If Will didn't have his kid with him, I'd give you a taste of your own medicine.' Arran cracked his knuckles.

'No, Arran.' Rhona grabbed him.

'I'd like to see you try.' Calum's eyes flickered.

'Let's just go.' She tugged Arran away, dragging him past Calum and Will, not looking at either of them.

'What's your problem?' Arran grumbled, shaking her off and stalking down the track. She kept her gaze low. Tears welled.

'I don't want a fight.'

She'd made her choice and left with her brother – again. Their family was still together. She was still part of their unit and Calum was safe from their wrath, for a while anyway. But her heart was back at the trench, lying trampled in the mud.

Chapter Twenty-Four

Calum

Calum picked up a rock and hurled it towards the sea. 'Aargh!' He clenched his fists. If Will wasn't there with little Angus he would have fallen to his knees and roared.

'Calum, what is going on?' Will's brow furrowed. 'First the wedding, now this. You still haven't explained why you walked out yesterday and went AWOL.'

'Yes, I did. I told you I wasn't feeling well.'

'Oh, come on, Calum. You're never ill.'

'Just leave me alone.' He didn't turn around. How could he face him? For a few glorious weeks, love had filled his soul. He'd learned how to give and receive it. But he didn't deserve it. He played second fiddle to Arran at school, now it was the same again. Rhona had made her choice.

'I'm not going anywhere,' Will said. 'You wouldn't have come on a walk with me if you'd really wanted to be alone. So, here I am.'

'Walking is fine but I'm not in the mood for small talk.'

'Ok then, instead of small talk, how about some big talk. Spit it out. Tell me what the hell's going on.'

Calum put his finger to his lips. 'Shh. Language in front of Angus.'

Will pulled a face. 'He's fast asleep. You can say what you want. He won't wake up until we get home.'

The thumping rage in Calum's head was receding but not enough. He rubbed his temple, trying to dispel it. 'I just...' he began but couldn't go on. The ache in his heart expanded, engulfing him with pain. He gripped his temples and forced his breathing to remain even.

'Calum.' Will rested his hand on his shoulder and Calum screwed his eyes shut. 'Arran's a dick. He always was. I won't ever forget what he did. At the time I was too shocked to make sense of it but now I know he's not worth it.'

'It isn't him.'

'Rhona then? What's happened? Has she scuppered the dig or something?'

'No. The dig's finished and so are we.'

'What do you mean? Were you and Rhona ever a thing?'

'Uh-huh.'

Will shook his head, barely concealing a grin. 'I had my suspicions. I saw the way you looked at each other.'

After working so hard at mastering his anger, he couldn't mask his feelings for Rhona. Whenever he was with her his behaviour gave him away. Of course Will had seen it. They'd been friends for so long. 'More fool me for trusting a Lamond.'

'So, what happened. Were you seeing her?'

'On her terms, or terms we agreed. I see it now.' What a great gift hindsight was. 'She was never going to choose me. It was fine when we were hushed up and she could hide me. I was her guilty secret. Just like Arran. He used to be my best friend until he got too cool, then he only spoke to me when no one else was about.'

'How could I forget? Stupid prick. It was my fault you fell out in the first place.'

'No, Will. It was his. I could take him pushing me around but I couldn't stand back and let him hurt you anymore. It had gone too far. He hurt one too many people I cared about.'

'I wish I'd had the nerve to do something myself but with his dad being a teacher...'

'He thought he was above the law.'

'I appreciate what you did. I was scared at the time but everyone wants a friend like you when the chips are down. You stuck up for me like no one ever had... Or has since.'

'And I'd do it again but that's the problem. It's in me.'

'No, Calum. What you did was the last straw.'

'But I got so carried away. I could have killed him.' He threw back his head and rubbed his face, erasing the vision of Arran's prone figure at the bottom of the stairs.

Will slung his arm over Calum's shoulder. 'But you didn't. You stopped. It was adrenaline and teenage hormones. Nothing like it has ever happened again. You did what you had to do to make sure of it. These days you're in control. You're the master of control, honestly, there's no one quite as poker-faced as you. You've found better ways to solve conflict.'

Was that true? He'd tried so hard. When he'd hurt Arran, it was spur of the moment, a culmination of anger built over months. The sickening agony after the event would never leave him.

He'd channelled his anger into karate and found shrewd ways to buy properties. Occasionally his temper got the better of him but he never lashed out physically. Pushing up rents had become his weapon of choice. Even that wasn't really him – Rebekah had called him out on it last year. 'Some days, I don't even know who I am.' Rhona had unlocked the man he wanted to be. The one who could love, be a partner, a husband, a father. He had all that inside him, hiding behind what he'd done and what he was capable of.

'You're Calum Matheson. You've built an empire and a reputation.'

'But it's not me.'

'It's part of you and there's nothing wrong with that.'

'I've made so many mistakes.'

'Who hasn't?' Will said. 'That's life. But don't let this be another one. Go after Rhona.'

'No. I can't. It's over.' That would be the mistake this time, chasing a dream that could never come true. 'She made her choice. I'm not crawling around grovelling, only for her to reject me the next time one of her family members comes into the room.'

Will tutted and looked away. 'Honestly, Calum, sometimes you're so stubborn. Give her a chance.'

'I already have.'

'Then give her another one. Maybe she needs more time. She's not an irritating tenant, she's someone you care about. That was a tough situation she was in. She didn't want the two of you going for each other. That wasn't her choosing Arran over you. That was her keeping the peace. Don't punish her for that. Go to her. Try.'

Calum patted Will on the back and sighed. 'You're a kind friend, Will. But if I go there, we'll go round and round in circles and nothing will happen. Her family hate me and there's no getting round that. If I break her family so we can see each other, do you think that'll make a solid start to a relationship? She'll hate me for it.'

'Oh, Calum, Calum, Calum. You're not just a stubborn ass, you're a right cynic as well. What are you afraid of?'

'I'm not afraid of anything.'

Will tilted his head.

Yeah, yeah. Of course he was afraid. What if she rejected him out and out? Leaving as the disgruntled martyr was easier than being sent packing straight to his face. 'I can't, I just can't.' He strode towards the site exit, Will hot on his heels.

After so much love over the past couple of months, he couldn't bear the tension creeping into his shoulders, his chest, his stomach. The thought of returning to 'normal' set a nauseous wave rising in his gut, but it was the only way. Pull out the poker face, encase his heart in an ice shield, keep people at arm's length and go.

Will bleeped open his maroon people carrier as soon as they got through the gate and Calum jumped into the passenger seat while Will settled Angus in his car seat. Any dreams Calum had harboured about this kind of life for himself were up the spout. A vague remnant of a tattered dream fluttered before him. He was clicking a little bundle of giggly cuddles into the back of his 4X4 and Rhona was on the other side, strapping in a miniature of herself, all blonde curls, big blue eyes and rosy cheeks. Their boot was stuffed full and a roof box packed to bursting point was clamped to the rails. Dad-Calum and Mum-Rhona were taking the kids on holiday. A bitter laugh almost split through his foul mood. Like any of that had the tiniest chance of being real. A Matheson and a Lamond together. How could he even have thought it?

He slumped back into the seat and Will hopped in beside him.

'Are you sure you don't want me to stop when we pass her house?' Will said. 'I'll stay in the car so you can chat.'

'No.' Calum held up a hand. 'Enough. Please.'

He just wanted to go home. Hopefully Arran and Rhona would leave the island and never trouble him again.

Chapter Twenty-Five

Rhona

Rhona's insides froze. *Shit.* Anne Matheson was across the road talking to someone. She'd turn around any second. *I can't let her see me. She might murder me.*

Taking Kirsten's arm, Rhona pulled her along the brightly painted main street in Tobermory, past the touristy shops, hoping the parked cars would shield her. The door to the Blue Whale Café was in sight. She tripped up the step as she went in.

'What is going on?' Kirsten closed the door behind them. 'Are you ok?'

'Fine, yes. Let's get a seat.' She spied a free table near the counter. Thank god the window seats were taken. She didn't want to be in full view. But what if Calum's mum was on her way over for a coffee? Rhona picked up the large menu and propped it at the edge of the table, ducking below it.

Kirsten's face creased. 'Are you sure you're ok?'

'No,' Rhona whispered. 'I'm not. Well, I am… But… There's something I need to talk to you about.'

The clink of spoons and cups seemed to hush. Rhona peeked over her menu wall. Was everyone listening?

'What?' Kirsten frowned and twisted her long dark hair over one shoulder.

Rhona leaned in. 'Calum.'

'Oh, I see.' Kirsten raised an eyebrow. 'You still crushing on him?'

Rhona propped her chin on her hand with a slow exhale. Confession time had arrived. 'It's a lot worse than that. A lot.'

'Oh no. What's happened? Another fall out?'

'No. Well, maybe. It's my fault. I've been seeing him in secret.' She kept her voice low.

'Wait... What? You have?'

Cha hadn't blabbed on messenger then. How well behaved. First time for everything. 'Yes.'

'Ok. That's not what I expected.'

Rhona flexed her toes inside her flat pumps, her limbs were heavy and achy. 'Don't get excited. It hasn't worked out well.'

'Because of the family feud thing?'

'Partly. I mean, things were going great. Like really great. I like him. Really, really, really like him. In fact, he even said...' She rocked her head from side to side, hoping Kirsten could mind read. 'That he loved me.' A lump accompanied the words to her throat. Rhona fanned her face, flapping away the pesky prickles rising in her nose and throat.

'Did he? Wow.'

'And I believed him.'

'So, what happened?'

'I bumped into him when I was with Arran and they got angry with each other. Calum wanted me to tell Arran about us there and then, but I couldn't. I needed them to get away from each other. I didn't want them to have another fight. So, I left. I know he's furious, but what can I do?'

'Can't you explain to your family about him?'

'How can I?' Rhona grasped her throat. Maybe throttling herself would help. 'It's like I have to decide but I can't.'

'There's no easy answer.'

'They keep telling me Calum's a brute and he's violent. Maybe it's true. He's always been gentle and kind with me but I've heard so many stories about him. Just the other week I saw him tackling bigger guys at karate and winning. He's a black belt for god's sake. He's trained to fight.' She stopped talking as the server came and took their order. Sucking on her lip, she waited.

Kirsten handed back the menus and the server moved back to the till. 'Just because he's good at karate doesn't mean he's violent.'

'But you know what happened with Arran and him at school?'

'Yeah... But...'

'What?' Rhona said. 'You didn't see what Arran looked like after it happened.'

'That's true. I only know what Beth told us.'

'What did she say?'

'She said that Arran, sorry...' Kirsten pulled a face.

'Tell me. All I know is Arran's version and I'm not sure I believe it.'

'From what Beth said, Arran was getting too big for his boots and acting all cool...' Kirsten fiddled with her napkin.

'Please, tell me.'

'Well, your dad was a teacher, so Arran pretty much got away with everything at school – no one dared say anything.'

'How could I forget? It was so awkward with him working there. Remember, you used to hide when he came to pick me up from your house.'

'Yes.' Kirsten smirked.

'But sorry, carry on.'

'So, remember, Calum had that terrible acne?'

'Yup.'

'Well, Arran started to disown him. Calum kind of withdrew. But Beth said Arran didn't just avoid him, he took the piss out of him, calling him names and being really horrible. He picked on all of them at one time or another. There was a girl he liked, Hannah, and Arran—'

'He snogged her to annoy Calum. I heard about that.'

'Then Arran dumped her. He teased her and stuff. Beth said Calum was fuming because he heard Arran calling her a slut. Then Arran started picking on Will. He pushed him about, called him names and taunted him. Will couldn't stop him and Arran kept going for him, trying to be funny but actually hurting him. Then Calum snapped. He punched Arran, then kicked him in the chest and knocked him down the stairs.'

Rhona sank her head into her hand. 'It sounds horrific.'

'Beth was traumatised watching it... I was shocked even hearing it. That's why I remember the story so well. I thought you knew... Sorry.'

'Not that version. Arran told Mum and Dad that Calum had jumped him on the stairs and it was unprovoked.' Rhona rubbed her face. 'I should have known Arran had more to do with it than he let on. Calum shouldn't have done it but it makes more sense now.'

'I think they were a bit scared of him after that.'

'I bet they were.' She'd seen Calum unleash his power in combat. And, yes, it was a scary sight. She rapped the table. 'I've noticed something this week I hadn't clocked before: my brother can be so full of himself. But my mum and dad think the sun shines out of his arse.' She gave a rueful laugh as she said it. 'But I need to do something about that.'

'What? Watch the sun rising from his backside?'

'No. Put him in his place. Put all of them in their place.' She'd been their baby for too long, listening to her sisters' verbal sparring and Arran's boasts, never getting involved, except to beg them to be nice to each other, or help them out of trouble. But not this time. Arran had got himself out of this for long enough. She couldn't sit back and hope it would mend itself.

'How are you going to do that?'

'I'm not sure.'

'Probably best to be direct. Just spit it out.'

Kirsten dropped Rhona back at her parents' house later in the afternoon. Her heart thudded nineteen to the dozen. *I have to do this. I have to do this.* She repeated the words over and over. The writhing sensation in her stomach vied for her attention and she inhaled a fortifying breath. Arran first. He was the one most likely to be there. She pushed open the main door. Ahead, through the open interior door, she spied him in the kitchen. A couple of steps in and his voice boomed out, laughing. She peered around the door. Alister sat at the table with his book and Arran was gesticulating as he told Judy a story. He didn't stop or make any sign of acknowledgement as Rhona entered, he just beamed at their mum, flashing his shiny teeth.

Rhona's ears were ringing. The easiest thing would be to slip up to her room and hide as she did when her sisters fought. Much easier to hide away and let the war go on around her without interfering. If she said what she wanted to, walls would crash down around her. Did she dare start the tremors? What if it split their family forever?

I have to do this.

Arran finally stopped talking and Judy laughed. Rhona's heart missed beat after beat. How could she do this? *But I have to.*

'Mum, Dad...' Blood raced to her head, singeing her cheeks. 'Arran.'

'What?' He leaned his forearms on the back of a chair.

'Is something wrong?' Judy poured boiling water into a cup. 'You look like you need a coffee. Shall I make you one?'

'No thanks. I have to tell you all something.'

Alister glanced up from his book.

Rhona swallowed and tried to draw in a breath; it rattled in her lungs. If she'd had the nerve to do this back in Crete and approached the directors immediately about Annike, she might have got somewhere with her complaint, but she'd shied away from it. She couldn't afford to do that now.

'What about?' Judy frowned, her mug poised at her lips.

'Calum Matheson.'

'Fuck's sake,' Arran muttered. 'What's he done?'

'Language.' Alister slapped his book on the table and glared at Arran.

Rhona clenched her fists at her sides. 'I've been seeing Calum for several weeks. And I don't mean at work.'

'You what?' Arran clutched the back of the chair.

Judy grabbed a seat and sunk into it. 'Good god.' She pressed her fingers to her forehead. 'Why?'

'Why do you think?' Rhona said. 'I like him. We like each other.'

'No way.' Arran shoved the seat and turned away, ruffing up his hair. 'Just no way. What has the creep done? Are you pregnant? Is he blackmailing you? I will fucking kill him if he's done anything to you.'

'No, Arran. He isn't a creep and he isn't a criminal.'

'This is ridiculous.' He held his hand to the top of his head, glowering and grating his teeth.

'It really is,' Judy said.

'Rhona.' Alister's voice was calm but stern. 'If you choose to forget what he did to your brother that's your business but I can't forget. I will never forget. I was a teacher in the school. How can I forget being called to the office to find him there beaten and bruised? Calum Matheson is an animal.'

'He could have killed Arran,' Judy said. 'I still wish we'd pressed charges.'

'What stopped you?' Rhona said.

'Arran didn't want to, which was big of him.'

'He didn't dare show face in school ever again,' Alister said. 'He doesn't even have high school leaving qualifications. He's a wheeling and dealing villain who makes money out of people's misfortune. I hoped he'd find remorse himself but—'

'He has,' Rhona said.

'Ha.' Arran scoffed. 'I don't know what lies he's told you—'

'He hasn't told me any lies.' Rhona seized the back of a chair, steadying herself. 'But you have.' She looked slowly at him. 'Why don't you tell them why he attacked you? And why you didn't want them to press charges.'

'It doesn't matter why,' Judy said.

'Yes, it does.' Rhona dug her nails into her palm. 'Tell them, or I will.'

Arran shrugged. 'I don't remember.'

'You were a bully.' Heat stung her neck and burned her throat, but she ploughed on. 'You used to be his friend, then he stopped being cool enough for you. Instead of leaving him alone though, you goaded him and teased him about his acne. You stole a girl you knew he liked, then dumped her and taunted her. And you hurt another of his friends. Calum could deal with you hurting him, but not other people. That's why he did it. You didn't want to press charges in case the truth came out and you were found guilty too. Guilty of hurting a lot more people than Calum.'

Judy's cheeks glowed and her hand shook as she reached for her coffee mug. 'Calum is still a dangerous man. Nothing changes that.'

'Is that true?' Alister zeroed in on Arran. 'You didn't bully him, did you?'

Arran rolled his eyes.

'Arran? You weren't bullying people, were you?'

'Yes, he was. And you worked at the school, so no one dared say anything.' Rhona looked back at Arran's surly face. 'They were scared you'd tell Dad and they'd fail maths or he'd have them suspended for something.'

'Oh, for fuck's sake. It was years ago. I was friends with Calum but he was the kid who had everything. He lived in that old house but he was an only child and his parents bought him whatever he wanted. He didn't have to share between siblings. And Will Laird was his crony, always telling people to be nice and leave him alone. Ugh!' Arran threw up his hands. 'They annoyed me. I was here with three sisters always having to compete for something.'

'Compete?' Judy said. 'We've always supported all of you.'

'We didn't raise you to be a bully,' Alister said.

'I told you, it was years ago. I grew out of it, so let's just forget it,' Arran said.

'You're right,' Rhona said. 'It was a long time ago. And what Calum did to you was a long time ago too. I'm sure he's not proud of it. If he didn't go back to school, it tells me he was ashamed. But he didn't sit around and waste away. He's successful because he took a gamble and it paid off. He's not dodgy or shady. He told me how he got his first property and how that started him off. Jealous people have made the rumours.' What reason did she have to doubt him? Her own insecurities had made her wary but her heart was right. She was sure.

Alister tapped his finger on the table.

'I can't tell any of you what to do,' Rhona continued. 'But I don't want to stop seeing him.' He might not want to see her after the other day but she was ready to take that chance. 'I don't want it to break up our family but that's my choice. You can either be with me or against me, but I won't change my mind.'

Judy looked at Alister, her eyebrows raised and her lips curved down. 'I don't know what to say.'

'I can't believe how you misled us.' Alister shook his head at Arran.

'Then why don't we forgive?' Rhona said. 'Forgive both Arran and Calum.'

'I'm not sure how we do that,' Alister said.

'That's up to you.' Rhona would have enough trouble convincing Calum she wanted him. But she had to, even if it meant rerouting her whole world.

Chapter Twenty-Six

Calum

Throwing kicks at the grappling dummy was punishing. Calum lurched back, then reeled forward. Each time he caught it, he imagined Arran's smug face and his crass words. *Kick. Punch. Punch.*

'Oh, Christ.' He threw himself onto the floor and lay on his back, rubbing vigorously at his temples. *Seriously. I'm as bad as everyone says.* He must be. Why else would he have the urge to crush Arran? Urges like this hadn't hit him for a long time. But Arran was back and he was the obstacle blocking Calum's path to Rhona.

He rocked into a sitting position and leapt to his feet. These workouts helped burn off some of the tension before he went to the office. He showered in scalding water, easing away the remaining stress in his body.

It was less than a mile from his flat in Tobermory but he took his car. Days rarely went by without a call to go somewhere. He had to be ready.

As he left, he pocketed his mobile in his blazer, recalling the first day Rhona had turned up here. Every day for weeks after, she'd dropped in to watch his practises and eat dinner. They'd spent hours kissing, cuddling and making love. His nerve ends fired up at the memories and he rubbed his chest; his heart was split clean in two.

He took his flask into the converted container with him, suspecting he'd be called out early. The Gruline tenants were still complaining about the slightest thing. He dumped the flask on the spare desk and set the kettle to boil. His long-term plans had included getting an admin assistant to work here alongside him but that hadn't happened yet. There was work enough and he could afford to pay for it but he wasn't sure he wanted someone here with him. Solitude was his friend – for the most part. He unpacked his laptop and opened it on his desk, facing the glass doors with the view of the trees. His temples pounded. Had he been unfair like Will suggested? Should he give Rhona a chance? And if he did, could he trust himself?

An urge to call her fired inside him and he grabbed his phone. A car pulled up outside, a door banged and Calum dropped the phone on the desk. What should he say?

He clicked open an email, scanning down, taking nothing in. A knock reverberated from the door. He raised his eyes over the screen. No way. His whole body tensed, only his blood was moving, making its presence known by thundering in his ears. The face staring through the glass was one he never wanted to see again. He leaned back, clenching his fists until his nails gouged his palms.

The French door opened slowly and Arran Lamond peered around. 'Can I, er, come in?' His gaze darted from Calum's face to the floor.

Calum stared at him, biting the inside of his lip. *What the hell?* Was there a gang of heavies around the corner waiting to jump him? He folded his arms and leaned back. 'What do you want?'

'We need to talk.' Arran ran his palm down the leg of his jeans. 'Can I come in or do you want me to say it on the doorstep?'

'That depends,' Calum trained his gaze on him, 'on what you want to say. If it's something inflammatory, then save it and leave. If it's something constructive, then... well...' He flicked his pointer finger, gesturing for Arran to come in. Would he? Or swear a lot then bugger off.

Skimming his hand over his hair, Arran crossed the threshold, then folded his arms. He glanced around, his chest heaving. He opened his mouth. Nothing. Looking down, he shuffled his feet.

'What's this about?' Calum steepled his fingers and leaned forward.

Arran huffed out a sigh. 'I need to say some stuff.'

'Oh yeah?' *Here we go.*

'About what happened when we were at school.'

'Right.' Calum summoned his poker face. He was well practised at it. Thanks to the man in front of him.

'It was bad shit.' Arran kept his eyes fixed on the far wall behind the spare desk.

'Too right it was.'

Arran bowed his head.

'Of course I regret my actions,' Calum said. 'But I'm not going to apologise. You were a bully and you had to be stopped. I should have gone about it differently.' He hadn't meant to hit him so hard but the overpowering desire to punish him after months of supressed pain had reared inside him and erupted alongside a potent cocktail of teenage hormones.

'Yeah, yeah.' Arran threw up his hands.

'So, is that it?'

'No. I didn't play fair. I shouldn't have picked on Will.'

'It wasn't just Will.'

'Or Hannah. Or you. Or anyone. I was an idiot.'

'Uh-huh.' Calum nodded. 'Why are you telling me this now?'

'Rhona heard... your side of things from a friend and told my parents.'

'My side of things?' The truth?

'Yup. I guess I didn't want people to know about my part in it.' Arran glanced at the floor, then slowly raised his eyes to Calum. 'What happened afterwards got out of hand. This war between our families.'

'I had nothing to do with that. Your family believed I was the bully and made sure that was the story that got spread around.'

'Yeah.'

'Nothing can make that go away.'

'Maybe we could...' Arran ruffed up his hair. 'You know?'

'Nope.' Calum leaned his elbow on the desk, rubbing his fingertips together. 'I've no idea why you're here. What do you want from me?'

'Nothing.' Arran swallowed, his Adam's apple bobbing. 'I'm trying to apologise, you know. Sorry and all that.' He threw out his palms and pulled a *what-do-you-say?* face.

Calum snorted and leaned back. 'Right. Just like that? Sorry and it all goes away?'

'Na. It's just a word, not a magic wand.'

'Too right.'

'But it's a start, right?'

Calum lifted a pen and fidgeted with it, turning it over. Something about this was off. 'Where has all this come from?'

'Rhona.'

Rhona. Yes. It had to be Rhona. She was behind this. Kind, caring, affectionate Rhona. The peacemaker. But this? Why? 'What did she say?'

'She told me about you and her.'

Heat burned Calum's neck. 'Right.'

'If that's what she wants... Well...'

'What does she want?'

'You, apparently.'

'She said that?' Calum crossed his arms. Was it possible? *She still wants me?*

'She said she'd made her choice. She called me out.'

'Right.' Words weren't coming easily. What did all this mean?

'It's time we try and put things straight.'

'We?'

'My parents have gone to see your parents.'

'They what?'

'Yup.'

'And Rhona knows about this?'

'She's gone with them.'

Calum ruffled the short hairs at his forehead. Rhona had made her choice. Really, him? His pulse skipped along. It could be ok. His focus flitted over the shelves of files containing his property information. He had plenty to offer in a material sense. He'd never doubted that. But Rhona didn't care about any of that. If she wanted him, it was because of what they had when they were together. The deep-rooted desire to believe it was something special forced its way out.

'Cool.' Calum's fingers twitched, then he stood and pushed out his hand. 'Should we shake?'

Arran stared at it for a moment before taking it. 'A truce?'

'Ok.' Calum shook briefly then let go.

As soon as Arran left, Calum pulled out his phone and called his mum.

'Oh my god, Calum,' she said. 'We have just had the strangest visit.'

'The Lamonds?'

'Yes. I'm in shock. My shift starts in half an hour but I might need to lie down.'

'What did they say?'

'They apologised and said they hadn't fully understood the circumstances of what happened when you were at school. I shouted a bit, then Judy and I had a good cry. It was so emotional. Even now I might go again.' She sniffed. 'Has Arran been to see you? They said he was heading that way.'

'Yes, he just left.'

'And how did that go?'

'It was ok.'

'Oh, god. I don't know what to make of it.'

'Did you see Rhona?'

'Yes, she was here, she didn't say much. She looked upset. I was angry with her parents before... well, the floodgates opened.'

'You know I really care about her?'

'Yes, sweetheart. Did I scare her off at the karate? I think I might have.'

'No, it wasn't you.'

'I was so convinced she would let you down. But now I'm not sure. I'm not sure about anything. Your dad's in shock too. He hasn't spoken for the last ten minutes.'

'Just take it easy.' Calum fiddled with his pen again. 'No one's asking you to be best buddies, only to be civil.'

'It's the oddest feeling after all these years.'

'I need to talk to Rhona. Did she go straight home?'

'I'm not sure. I don't think so though. It's a bit of a blur but I think Judy said Rhona was leaving to set up a dig site.'

'What?' Calum's heart sank to his shoes. If she had a site to set up, it wouldn't be on the island. How could it be? Had she set this up only to disappear? Maybe she didn't believe he'd accept the apology or give in after stubbornly hating her family for so long. Was this her parting gift?

'I think that's what she said.'

'Ok, take it easy, Mum. I've got stuff to do.'

As soon as he ended the call, he tapped out a message.

CALUM: Are you there? Please call me. X

Concentrating was impossible. His eyes kept dipping to his phone. No reply. She could be on a remote site or travelling. She worked all over the world. Who was to say where she was or where she was heading?

For the first day in a long time, nobody phoned. Nobody called him out and Calum filled the hours attending to admin. His phone was so ominously quiet, he restarted it after lunch. Nothing from Rhona. When he locked up at five, he still hadn't heard anything. Should he drive to her house? But if she was on a dig, she might be away for several days.

Back home, he logged into Facebook. He rarely used it or posted anything but he'd responded to her friend request some weeks ago. Her feed was full of archaeology-related pictures, shares and links – even a picture of the Kilnarkie dig. But nothing since last week. Nothing to give any clue of where she was or what she was doing now.

He gazed out over the colourful village from his lofty window. This view was great but part of him longed to be on the other side of the island, looking out on the setting sun at Kilnarkie. That was the kind of place to put down roots and build a forever home.

His phone lit up and his heart bounced.

RHONA: I hope you and Arran got on ok today. I always trusted you and knew you'd never hurt anyone. I believe what you did at school was a culmination of events. I'm sorry it's shaped your life like this but maybe things can turn a corner for our families now. I really hope so.

I'm also sorry to have to add this...

Calum's pulse quickened at the words.

... but I was looking back over my research and noticed something important at Kilnarkie. You need to come over ASAP. Bring a change of clothes, this might get dirty. It's urgent. X

His shoulders tightened and he clenched his fist. What? That was where she'd been. And why? He responded briefly.

CALUM: Ok, on my way x

A heavy weight impeded his breathing as he drove along the twisty roads, taking the corners a little too fast. Why would she go back to the dig? What had she seen that had prompted it? And what the hell had she found? He'd packed a change of clothes but why did he need them? She didn't want him to help her dig something up, did she? Was it something huge? Something that would prevent him building the house he desperately wanted? The one he wanted not just for himself but for both of them. Would she want that too? Was he too late? Had he blown his chance with her?

He crunched the car into the quarry car park at the site entrance and jumped out. The ground yielded soft and dry underfoot as he made his way over the grass. A faint smell of woodsmoke drifted in the air. The trench came into view. Not far. Rhona should be visible too. Where was she? He moved to the edge and peered in. Exactly as it was before. He put his hands in his pockets and frowned. What was going on?

Chapter Twenty-Seven

Rhona

The sticks glowed red in the pit Rhona had dug. She prodded them, hoping for a little more flames. What a pitiful attempt compared to the blaze Jay had got going on the beach in Crete. A lifetime ago. Jay and Annike still occasionally appeared on Facebook, posting pictures of their current digs.

Rhona had spent the latter part of the day penning a strongly worded email to Annike's latest project director. It may never get her research back but it finally got it off her chest. If it sounded whiny or like sour grapes, so be it, but she'd tried. Simon had agreed to back her up.

And now she'd set the ball rolling with her family and the Mathesons, the only future she could see had Calum in it – if he wanted that. And she was ready to sell it to him. She'd set up her bivvy tent and her pulse raced as she checked inside. Recreating an Iron Age home in a few hours wasn't possible, but this had the ambience she was after. Small and cosy. Sleeping mats replaced straw floors and fleece blankets would be softer than animal skins.

Crawling on her knees to the edge of the bush, Rhona peered out and her skin prickled. Calum was there, standing at the trench. How had she not heard the car? Brain fuzz! Ever since the meeting with Ron and Anne, her world had been spinning on double time. Anne had been furious, ranting and screaming, but Ron had calmed her and they'd got talking. Judy had cried. Anne cried. Alister had spoken calmly but Rhona had seen him twitching. It might be a short-lived ceasefire. Years of hurt couldn't be swept away in a few minutes, but it was a start. Time would tell.

Now for Calum. Rhona swallowed, rubbing her palms together. This was it. As she stood, he pulled out his phone and turned the opposite way. His voice carried on the wind though she couldn't hear exactly what he was saying. He pushed his finger into his free ear, as if blocking the noise of the wind and waves. Head bowed, he paced and chatted. Then, no! He started to walk away, gesticulating. His voice sounded grim. She pushed forward, she had to go after him. He was trudging towards the exit.

'Calum!' Her shout was carried on a sharp gust.

He kicked the ground, his phone still pressed to his ear. A frown creased his face as he turned. Of course he was annoyed. He thought he was coming to see something important, something which might ruin his building dreams. What she had to show him was important but hopefully it wouldn't ruin anything. He ended the call and squinted towards her.

She edged towards him, biting her lip, not sure what to do with her hands.

'What's going on?' The crease in his forehead deepened. 'What have you found?'

'Myself.' She pulled a shrug alongside her smile.

He shook his head. 'I don't follow.'

'I lost my way before I came home. Then you came along and made me believe again.'

'I didn't do that.'

'Indirectly you did. I've always been terrible at making up my mind and trusting my own judgement. I tried to please everyone, even if it meant going along with things I didn't like. But I realised I couldn't do that. I couldn't go along with my family and their treatment of you. Not when I feel so much for you.'

He fiddled with his wristwatch. 'You already know what I feel for you.'

'I do. And I should have said it before. I love you too. There's never been anyone like you.'

From several feet apart, they stared at each other, then at the same moment, he opened his arms and she pounced on him, flinging her arms around his neck. He swung her off her feet and she giggled, dangling in mid-air.

'And you trust me?' he said.

'No one more so.'

They smiled and gazed at each other for a long moment. 'So, why the suspense?' He set her back on her feet. 'You had me freaking out. What am I here to see? Why do I need spare clothes?'

'Because you're not going home tonight, not to Tobermory anyway.'

'You want me to stay with your parents? Much as I love you and am thrilled with how you've started to heal things between our families, I'm not sure I'm ready to crash on them like that.'

'I meant we're staying here.'

'Here?'

'You want to live here, don't you?'

'I do. One day. I thought, maybe, well, it's early days but...'

'But what?'

'Maybe one day we might live here together.'

Warm bubbles fizzed through her chest, filtering into her veins and she beamed. 'I would love that. This place has called to me ever since I was little. Whoever lived here all those centuries ago carved out a perfect spot and the only other people who have lived here since are passing shepherds. We'll be the first people to make it our home for centuries.'

'For someone with such a scientific job, you really are a romantic soul.'

'And that's why...' She took his hand. 'We're going to spend our first night here in the style of our ancestors.'

'What?'

'Come see.' She tugged him down the hill where it plateaued close to the beach. She'd set up her camp in the sheltered lee of a row of scrubby bushes. Billowing smoke rose from her pathetic campfire.

'Are you burning my land?'

She giggled. 'Yup, well, hopefully the fire's working but I've never been that great at making them.'

As they reached the level ground, Calum scanned around first at the camp then turned to stare out to sea. 'It's awesome. All of it.'

'So, when the house is built,' Rhona stoked the fire, 'I see this as being a kind of terraced garden where we can sit of an evening.'

'Is that after you've dug it up?'

'Er... Yes.' She pulled out her lips and tried to look innocent.

Calum stepped forward, cupped her cheeks in his palms, dipped his head and kissed her. Rhona sighed into the kiss, letting out a little cry of delight as their souls reconnected. 'What's mine is yours. You can do anything you want here.' He dropped his eyelids, resting his forehead on hers.

'The first thing I'm going to do is immerse you in the Iron Age experience. I have food.' She indicated a basket next to the bivvy. 'And we have a bed.' She pulled back the canvas and Calum peered in.

'You want me to sleep in there?'

'That's the general idea.'

'You know I've never even been camping?'

'Until now, Mr Matheson. We're living on the land tonight. We can snuggle up and watch the stars.'

His gaze rose skywards and the light reflected in his sea-green eyes, twinkling like infinite possibility. 'Ok, Miss Lamond. Let's do it.'

Settled by the campfire, Rhona nuzzled into Calum. With August coming to a close, darkness rolled in by nine. Calum's arm lodged firmly around her and she kept as close as she could. His warmth was better than the dying fire against the evening breeze.

She tucked her fingers inside the lower edge of his sweater. 'This is nice, isn't it?'

'It really is.' He kissed the top of her head. 'I love you so much. I've been terrified you'd leave. Even now I'm not sure you don't think I'm a monster underneath.'

'Stop, Calum. You're not. Since I got to know you, I never thought that.'

'Thank you.' He ran his thumb over her cheek. 'But it doesn't change the fact that you have a job and a life that means you can't stay here permanently.'

'Yeah.' Glancing down, she sighed. She'd blocked her worries about that until she was sure Calum wanted her. Now they came flooding back. She didn't have a job except a few ad hoc research projects.

'But I might have a way around it... If you wanted to hear it.'

'Of course I do.'

'My job is basically maintaining the properties I own, managing rentals and looking for deals. If I hand over some of that to an assistant, I don't have to be here. I can work from anywhere as long as I have access to a phone. The stuff that has to be dealt with hands on is where the assistant would come in. So, I could travel with you wherever you need to go.'

Rhona sat up, breaking free of his hold. 'You'd do that?'

'Definitely.'

She pushed his knees flat and crawled onto his lap, straddling his hips, and resting her palms on his shoulders. 'You're the best.'

He gathered her against his chest. As she made contact with him, tingles shot through her. He kissed her gently, then broke off with a delicate tug on her bottom lip. A whimper escaped her and she closed her eyes. The dying fire cast a flickering glow over Calum's cheekbones and his aquiline features. 'I just want us to be together,' he said.

Rhona chased his mouth and when she caught it, she slipped her hands fully around his neck, pulling him closer, pushing her chest firmly into his. They were lost, meshed together. Rhona shuffled on top of him. 'Let's get inside.'

Together they crawled in, tugging off clothes. Calum reclined Rhona gently, barely breaking the kiss, and pulled the soft fleeces around them. The wind flapped the tent as Rhona lost herself in the darkness, the warmth of his embrace, the heat of his tongue, the softness of his lips. This was where she belonged.

Rhona couldn't open her eyes. Her breathing had calmed and Calum was still holding her close. His body rose and fell as she snuggled into him. He nuzzled into her hair. 'I've missed us.'

'Well, you don't have to miss us anymore.' Rhona slipped her arm over his tight waist. 'The thing is, I've been thinking.'

'When?'

'Obviously not in the last hour.' She winked. 'In general. My career has been disappointing for a while now. I'd like to break into consultancy and if I did, then I would live here most of the time and travel to research sites for a week or so at a time, rather than spending half the year away and only coming back for a few weeks.'

'Perfect.' Calum stroked her hair. 'You can do it. I've seen your work. I even have office space. We could share.'

'Can we? That would be amazing. And I might invest in the reconstruction software.'

'That's exactly what you have to do. You have such a talent, you need to use it. Let the world see what you're made of.'

She burrowed in close. 'I'm not sure what I expected to find when I came back but it definitely wasn't this.'

His chest vibrated with a laugh. 'Nope, this wasn't in my yearly plan either. But it's easily the best thing that's happened to me for a long time.'

Rhona let out a happy sigh. She'd found her heart and where it belonged. Of all the discoveries she'd made in her life, this was the most perfect.

Chapter Twenty-Eight

Calum

Blue skies stretched as far as the eye could see. Boats gleamed in the Tobermory marina, dazzling Calum. He squinted and clutched Rhona's hand. Maybe there would be a time when it didn't feel surreal walking like this with her but it wasn't today. People seemed to slow as they passed or do a double take, maybe they were muttering, 'Look, there's Calum Matheson, the miser, with Rhona Lamond. Wonder what he bribed her with.'

Will and Morven strolled beside them with baby Angus strapped in his carrier on his mum's chest. With the meeting he had coming up, Calum wouldn't have chosen this exact moment for a chat with his friend, but Will had spotted him on the street and there was no shaking him. He was in his usual talkative mood. Calum was used to it but nerves were building and the constant chit-chat wasn't helping.

'You two look so perfect.' Will grinned.

'Thanks,' Calum said. Rhona's cheeks bloomed and she smiled.

'I couldn't have picked someone better for you myself,' Will said. 'And believe me, I wanted to.'

'Yes, Will. I know. And now you don't have to.' Calum's focus strayed across the marina, seeking the Dawn Treader. Were his parents there yet? Were Rhona's? This could be a disaster in the making rather than the bonding trip Rhona had planned.

She squeezed his fingers. Without saying a word, her eyes said, *It'll be fine.*

He wanted to believe her but the hope in his heart wasn't completely divorced from the years of fear.

'I had a nice visit from Arran before he left,' Will said.

'Did you?' Rhona said.

Calum frowned. 'You didn't tell me that.'

Will wasn't one to hold a grudge. If Calum hadn't stepped in that day at school and Arran had succeeded in beating Will up, Will would probably have found a way to forgive and forget anyway. Even if Calum couldn't.

'You had other things on your mind.' Will waggled his eyebrows.

'What did he say?' Rhona asked.

'Ah, he apologised for stuff he said a long time ago. We were silly teenagers but it hurt. And I'm glad he came and spoke to me. I've always felt bad about it, like it was actually my fault.'

'No, Will. It's never the victim's fault.' Calum reached out and put his arm around Will's shoulder. 'He had no right to bully you like that, even if we were teenagers. Nor should I have reacted the way I did.'

Will chuckled. 'Ah, Calum, you always were a lot fiercer than me, quiet but strong, and the best mate I could have.'

A lump swelled in Calum's throat and he gave Will a pat. 'Thanks.'

'I'm so relieved it's worked out,' Rhona said.

'Let's hold off judgement until later.' Calum's gut roiled. 'This boat trip could go pear-shaped. Our families have been warring for a long time. It's a big ask, shoving them into a confined space together for the afternoon and hoping they'll get on like best buddies.'

'They wouldn't have agreed to do it if they didn't want to try,' Will said.

'Exactly,' Morven said. 'They both value their children and they want to do what's best for both of you.'

'Keep it short,' Will said. 'Just in case. You know, baby steps.'

Calum peeked at Rhona again.

She squeezed his hand. 'We can do this.'

'Listen,' Will said. 'Speaking of baby steps, and while we have you here, we have something to ask you.' He looked at Morven, who nodded, then at Calum.

'Oh yeah?' Calum frowned.

'We'd like you to be Angus's godfather.'

'Oh... Right. Wow.' Calum's chest swelled and Rhona hugged his arm. 'Yeah, sure I will. It's an honour.'

He embraced Will and they clapped each other on the back.

'Excellent,' Will said.

Calum gave Morven a peck on the cheek and ran his thumb over Angus's peach-fuzz head. 'I look forward to being your godfather, little man.'

They'd reached the entrance to the jetty and Rhona tugged on his arm. Standing by the boat were his parents, next to Alister and Judy. Calum swallowed. They were talking, though none of them appeared overly thrilled. Maybe this meeting would sink before they even got aboard.

'We should go,' he said.

'Good luck.' Morven took Will's arm. 'We'll leave you to it.'

Will cast his eyes towards the boat. 'Yes, good luck.'

'Come on, Will.' Morven dragged him away.

Calum and Rhona exchanged a look.

'Here goes,' she said.

'At least we've got each other. Though it'd be a lot easier if our families were onboard too.'

Together, they strolled hand in hand towards their parents. Numbness spread up Calum's arm and over his shoulders. He rolled them, bracing himself.

'Hey.' Rhona broke away from Calum and hugged everyone. Her infectious smile spread around the group. Feeling returned to Calum's fingers and he exhaled slowly.

'I'll steer her out the bay if you like,' Ron said. 'That'll give you a chance to be with your lovely lady.' He gave Calum a pat, smiling at them both like they were the most beautiful people he'd ever seen.

'Is that you pretending to do me a favour?' Calum asked.

'I like being at the helm,' Ron said.

'I wouldn't know where to start,' Alister said.

'If you want to learn, I'm sure Dad would help.' Calum mustered his best smile, pushing away the bad memories, forgetting this was his former maths teacher and instigator of so much hate over the years. This was a peace mission. And he wanted to prove himself worthy of Alister's daughter. Their parents' blessing wasn't necessary but it would make things much sweeter.

'Yes, I wouldn't mind seeing how it works.' Alister climbed into the cabin and disappeared behind Ron. Anne and Judy took seats on the deck and chatted with cheery faces. Anne was well practised in gossip and spent most of her day chatting to people in the shop, so she was no stranger to keeping a friendly conversation going.

Calum sidled up behind Rhona and wrapped his arms around her from behind. 'Do you think this is an act?' he whispered. 'Are they behaving like this to please us?'

'Maybe. But they're trying. I just hope they can keep it up.'

Calum tugged Rhona close, dipped in and kissed her on the cheek. 'I love you.'

She melted in his arms and he rocked her gently as the boat chugged out of the marina.

'I love you too but I do have one regret.'

'Do you?' Calum's heart prickled. What had he done wrong?

'I still haven't succeeded in one of my missions.' Rhona leaned back and smiled at him.

'Which is?'

'Getting you skinny dipping.'

Calum laughed and bent his head into her hair. 'Is that all? You had me seriously worried there... And wait a minute... You were going to get me to A: like history, B: get dirty and C: sleep with you in a bivvy. I've done all three.'

Rhona giggled. 'Ah no, when we went to Coll, I added that one.'

'No, you asked me if you could add it and I quite categorically said no.'

'Like you did with the other three?'

'Uh-huh... Like that.'

Rhona waggled her eyebrows. 'So, when are we doing it?'

'Let's do this trip first.'

'Really?'

He leaned in and claimed her lips, closing his eyes as he gently kissed her. 'Anything, Rhona. Anything for you.'

The sun splintered through the clouds and despite it being early September, the air was warm and balmy. They cruised around the bay and Ron anchored the boat in a picturesque spot with a view back to Mull, the mainland on the other side.

Calum clinked his lime soda on Rhona's glass, then his mum's. 'Couldn't ask for a better day.'

Anne patted his knee. 'I couldn't ask for a better boy.'

'Thanks, Mum.'

'And you're exactly the right girl for my boy.' She smiled at Rhona. 'I can see it in the way you look at each other. Perfect. Just perfect.' She wiped a tear away.

Judy sniffed beside her and did the same. Rhona leapt between the two of them and pulled them into a giant group hug.

Calum's chest was considerably lighter as they said goodbye later in the afternoon. 'That was better than I expected,' he said, as they strolled towards his apartment.

'I'm glad it's done though,' Rhona said. 'Hopefully that's paved the way for happier times ahead.'

Calum zapped open the car as they approached it. 'Let's hope.'

'Are we going somewhere?'

'Into the sea.'

'What? You mean it?'

'I promised, so let's do it.'

He drove to Kilnarkie and they ambled to the secluded beach in front of the dig site, holding hands and stopping for an occasional kiss. The sun was setting beyond, silhouetting the distant Isle of Coll where Rhona had first proposed skinny dipping.

'Ok.' Calum unzipped his Trespass jacket. 'Let's get it over with.'

'You're actually going to? Even though you don't even like getting your feet wet?'

'Yup.' He discarded his jacket, followed by his t-shirt. Rhona grinned, checking him out. He gave a little shrug. She'd seen it before but if it made her want to come back for more, who was he to complain? All thoughts of complaining or anything else were knocked out of the water when she mirrored him and pulled off her top. She was hotter than the infernos of hell and caused as much damage to his brain. Skinny dipping was slipping to the bottom of the list of things he wanted to do, but he wouldn't chicken out that easily. Simultaneously they slid out of their remaining clothes. Then... *What the?* She slammed herself against him, threaded her fingers through his hair and kissed him. Skinny dipping wasn't happening, not tonight. *But no, shit.* As soon as she'd started, she let go and ran for it. Calum threw back his head and let out an exasperated shout, then legged it after her.

Wherever she went, he was going too, and he wouldn't let anything push them apart ever again.

Epilogue

Rhona

Flutters of disjointed reality swooped through Rhona's tummy as she clung to Calum's hand. She was here, in Egypt. The place every archaeologist everywhere had to visit at least once in their lifetime.

November was a good time; the weather was warm but not as baking as during the summer and so far, the sunblock was holding.

Calum adjusted his panama hat. Coupled with his neat dark hair and brows it leant him a nineteen-thirties debonair style. Rhona beamed.

'What?' He frowned as she smirked at him.

'You're like the handsome cad from *Death on the Nile*.'

'Am I? Well, let's hope you don't end up as my latest victim.' He lifted an eyebrow and pulled an evil grin.

'Yikes. Are you the murderer?'

He wrapped his arm around her. 'Possibly, but until we find out, I'll be the rakish lover.'

She chuckled and poked him. 'That sounds more like it.'

From outside their hotel, they got on the charter bus bound for the great pyramid. Rhona pulled out her phone, leaned into Calum and snapped a selfie.

'We need a selfie on the bus?' he said.

'I'm having a record of everything and it's all going on Facebook.'

'Why?'

'Because Simon just messaged me.' He'd returned to Crete for the year and was working again with Annike.

'What did he say?'

'Annike's been demoted to the trenches.'

'I like where this is going.'

'She got fired for misconduct from the management job she got on the back of stealing my work last year.' Rhona smirked, scrolling onto Facebook. 'And I might be getting credited with the research after all.'

'Brilliant. You deserve it. You're amazing at what you do.'

She nudged him with a smile. 'Simon says she's lucky to have a job at all. And if Simon says, then it must be true.'

'And you're posting stuff on Facebook to annoy her.'

'Silly, isn't it?' She selected a range of pictures. 'I'm also posting them because I'm happy. Earlier this year, she almost ruined my career. Now, she's ruined her own and I've got so much to look forward to.' She gave his knee a squeeze.

'Karma.'

'Exactly. Though rubbing her nose in it is pretty mean. Maybe I shouldn't.'

'She probably won't even look, so you're not rubbing her nose in it, you're just celebrating. Celebrating us.'

She rested on his shoulder and he slung his arm about her as they watched for the pyramids.

'I didn't fully grasp how close to the city they were,' Calum said. 'Or how big they are.'

'They're huge. This is so awesome. Isn't it incredible they were built before the tiny little homestead at Kilnarkie? The people had the skills to do it.'

'It's unreal.'

The bus drew up and Rhona got to her feet. Calum waited for a few people to pass and get off first before taking Rhona's hand. Together they jumped off and goggled around.

'Wow.' Rhona's head was ready to explode at the sight of so much history.

Guards on camels and horseback trotted around, keeping people from getting too close.

'I take it we can't climb them?' Calum said.

'Would you want to?'

'Not really. I'll stick to looking.'

Hand in hand, they strolled around. The magic of being here pervaded every pore and Rhona tweaked her sun hat, closed her eyes and let the sun warm her face.

Calum's placed a kiss on the warm centre of her cheek. 'I'd never have thought to come here before I met you. So many things I'd never have done if it hadn't been for you.'

'Like cuddling.'

'Exactly.' He wrapped his arms around her. 'I'm sticking with you.'

'Good, because you're mine and I'm not letting you go.'

He smiled at her. The shadow of the great pyramid loomed ahead, pointing to the future. When they got home, she was ready to start a new business. Calum had arranged for construction to begin at Kilnarkie at the end of the month. The dream house would be built over the home of their ancestors and together they'd breathe a new future into the place.

He stroked his thumb over the shell tattoo on her shoulder. 'Maybe I should get a pyramid on mine.'

'I hated it when I first got it, now it's like my lucky charm.'

'It's so you.'

'Well, shells symbolise femininity, the womb and good fortune, so maybe it was a sign.'

He cupped his hands around her cheeks and pulled her in for another kiss. 'And surely pyramids mean something to do with prosperity.'

'And manhood.' She winked. 'Pyramids have strong foundations and they point upwards, striving for better things.'

'Sounds ideal.'

'So, together we have prosperity and good fortune.' She beamed up at him. 'And a strong foundation to grow a family.'

'I'd love that.' He nodded and gently stroked his palm over her tummy. 'I thought the opportunity to become a dad would pass me by and I accepted it, but now I want that for us. You, me and lots of babies.'

'Me too.'

She flung her arms around his neck. There was no rush but the knowledge that they were in this forever was enough to fill Rhona with deep contentment. Calum splayed his fingers on her back and swayed her gently. 'You're my everything, Miss Lamond.'

'And you're mine, Mr Matheson.'

As the bustle and chat of tourists rolled by, Calum and Rhona held fast. The rift between their families was healing and together they were free to pursue the rest of their lives, following in the footsteps of the past and chasing the promise of the future.

The End

MORE BOOKS BY MARGARET AMATT

Scottish Island Escapes

1. A Winter Haven

2. A Spring Retreat

3. A Summer Sanctuary

4. An Autumn Hideaway

5. A Christmas Bluff

6. A Flight of Fancy

7. A Hidden Gem

8. A Striking Result

9. A Perfect Discovery

10. A Festive Surprise

The Glenbriar Series

1. Stolen Kisses at the Loch View Hotel

2. Just Friends at Thistle Lodge

3. Pitching up at Heather Glen

4. Two's Company at the Forest Light Show

5. Highland Fling on the Whisky Trail

6. Snowdown at the Old Schoolhouse

7. Starting Over at the Crafty Bee Barn

8. A Surprise Proposal in the Rose Garden

9. Cutting it Neat for the Wedding

10. A Classy Affair in the Country

11. Mix Up under the Mistletoe

12. A Fresh Start on the Bridle Path

About the Author
Margaret Amatt

Margaret has told and written stories for as long as she can remember. During her formative years, she spent time on long walks inventing characters and stories to pass the time.

Writing books is Margaret's passion and when she's not doing that, she's often found eating chocolate, walking and taking photographs in the hills around Highland Perthshire. Those long walks still frequently bring inspiration!

It's Margaret's pleasure to bring you the Scottish Island Escapes series and The Glenbriar Series. These books are linked (both the two series have crossovers!) for those who enjoy inhabiting Margaret's world of stories but each book can be read as a standalone if you'd rather dip in and out.

You can find more information about Margaret on her website or by signing up for her newsletter.

www.margaretamatt.com

Acknowledgments

Thanks goes to my adorable husband for supporting my dreams and putting up with my writing talk 24/7. Also to my son, whose interest in my writing always makes me smile. It's precious to know I've passed the bug to him – he's currently writing his own fantasy novel and instruction books on how to build Lego!

Throughout the writing process, I have gleaned help from many sources and met some fabulous people. I'd like to give a special mention to Stéphanie Ronckier, my beta reader extraordinaire. Stéphanie's continued support with my writing is invaluable and I love the fact that I need someone French to correct my grammar! Stéphanie, you rock. To my lovely friend, Lyn Williamson, thank you for your continued support and encouragement with all my projects. And to my fellow authors, Evie Alexander and Lyndsey Gallagher – you girls are the best! I love it that you always have my back and are there to help when I need you.

Also, a thanks to the editors at Leannan Press for their work on this novel.

Of course a huge thank you goes to the readers who continue to support me in so many ways. I appreciate each and every one of you and hope that I can keep bringing you more books to enjoy! Big love.

Margaret XX

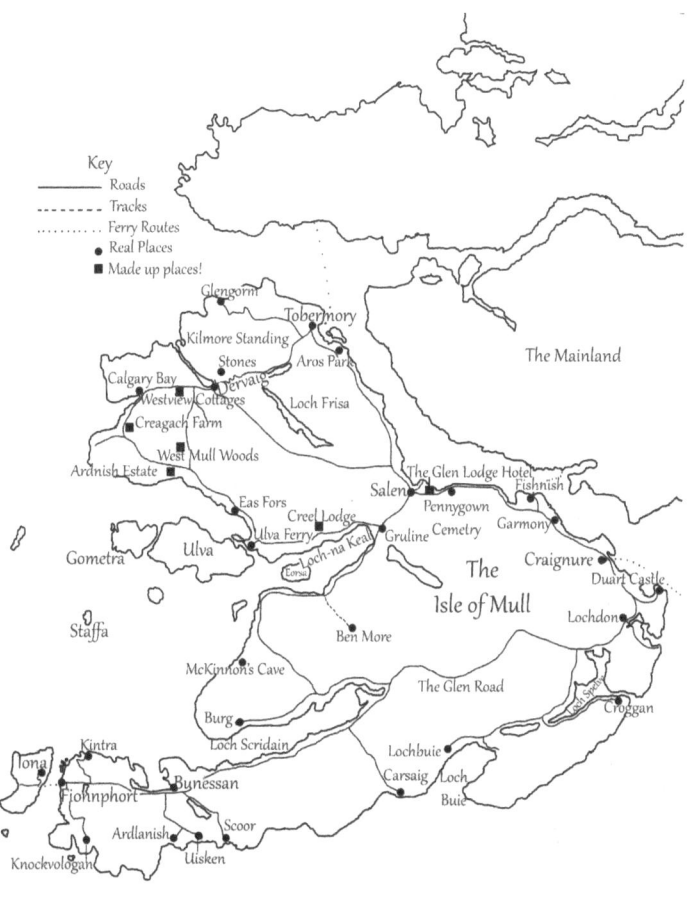

The Isle of Mull where the Scottish Island Escapes series is set

www.ingramcontent.com/pod-product-compliance
Lightning Source LLC
Chambersburg PA
CBHW011956090526
44590CB00023B/3748